ST. AUGUSTINE'S THEORY OF KNOWLEDGE: A CONTEMPORARY ANALYSIS

Intellectum valde ama.
Epistle 120
Be passionately in love
with understanding.

ST. AUGUSTINE'S THEORY OF KNOWLEDGE: A CONTEMPORARY ANALYSIS

BRUCE BUBACZ

Texts and Studies in Religion
Volume 11

The Edwin Mellen Press
New York and Toronto

Library of Congress Cataloging in Publication Data

Bubacz, Bruce.
    St. Augustine's theory of knowledge.

    (Texts and studies in religion ; v. 11)
    1. Augustine, Saint, Bishop of Hippo-Knowledge,
Theory of. 2. Knowledge, Theory of--History.
I. Title. II. Title: saint Augustine's theory of
knowledge. III. Series: Texts and studies in re-
ligion ; 11.
B655.Z7B8   121'.092'4   81-18754
ISBN 0-88946-959-8   AACR2

Texts and Studies in Religion ISBN 0-88946-976-8

        The Edwin Mellen Press
        P.O. Box 450
        Lewiston, New York   14092

Printed in the United States of America

For

Mary Elizabeth

Quid illam vocem nonne de visceribus cunctorum
patrum Cicero emisit ad filium, ad quem scribens ait,
"Solus es omnium, a quo me in omnibus vinci velim"?
Secundam Juliani Responsionem
Imerfectum Opus VI, 22

PREFACE

I have spent the past ten years becoming acquainted with St. Augustine. I have not been studying Augustine, and I have not been merely reading his works. I have joined the untold thousands who -- over the centuries -- have engaged this demanding, aggravating and enlightening genius. The experience has been, more than anything else, a dialogue, for Augustine doesn't simply tell you what he thinks. He forces you to consider what *you* think. He forces you to bring order to the confusion of your ideas, to consider various possibilities, and to prepare for a philosophical counterattack. Augustine is not simply a great philosopher; he is a great teacher.

Following Augustine's example, I have a confession to make. This work is not simply a treatment of Augustine's epistemology. It is also a response to those philosophers in what is called the "linguistic" or "analytic" tradition who dismiss the works of such God-centered philosophers as Augustine. This prudishness about religious issues is wide-spread in contemporary American philosophy. Many who style themselves "medievalists" focus upon the logic choppers of the middle ages -- the philosophers who wrote of abstruse, arcane, "technical" problems, problems that have nothing to do with the tensions and contradictions that human beings confront in their lives. This emphasis is not surprising, for much of contemporary philosophy is a self-sustaining, incestuous seminar in problems that few people ever encounter in their daily lives, and fewer still would take seriously. Our society has suffered because of this. Important questions -- questions that should be confronted with reason and intelligence -- are ignored by philosophers, and are left to those who will "solve" them through bigotry, superstition, ignorance, and rationalization.

Augustine is a teacher. He speaks to each of us. We may or may not agree with what he has to say about knowledge. But his methodology makes it necessary for us to disagree rationally.

This book is an account of what Augustine has said to me.

As with any work of scholarship, many people have helped me along the way.

Seale Doss was my first philosophy professor at Ripon College. His exciting teaching style and his provocative questions attracted me to philosophy. His integrity and excitement about ideas attracted me to him. We have become and remained friends for seventeen years. His continued interest in my work has been a great comfort to me.

At the University of Washington Kenneth Clatterbaugh taught me that the history of philosophy -- even what he called "antique philosophy" -- is an exciting area of research. Most philosophers say that an understanding of the history of our subject is essential for an understanding of the subject itself. Ken taught me the reason for this, and encouraged my research.

John Boler taught me the patterns, intricacies and methods of the philosophers of the middle ages. A human, decent, civilized man himself, John showed me that philosophy was all of these things as well -- that it need not be an intellectual bear garden. He guided my early research into Augustine.

My colleague Edward Walter has spent the past eight years reading, editing and -- most importantly -- encouraging my writing. In all of this he has been a

true and tireless friend, and has often kept me going
when I didn't want to. I could not have asked for a
better guide.

It is unlikely that I would have embarked on this
study of Augustine's epistemology without the encour-
agement of Mary Sirridge, Gareth Matthews and Frederick
van Fleteren. All three have read my work at various
stages, and all three have helped me to avoid large
mistakes.

The Augustinian Historical Institute and Villanova
University provided hospitality and a comfortable research environment during the summer of 1978. My work
was supported by a Younger Humanists Summer Stipend
from the National Endowment for the Humanities, and a
grant from the Office of Research Administration of the
University of Missouri-Kansas City. I am grateful to
these institutions for their invaluable assistance.

Finally, I would like to give special thanks to
Nanette Biersmith, who typed this work in its various
incarnations. I suspect that by now she has this book
memorized, but she never complained, worked diligently,
and offered many helpful suggestions.

I give my thanks to all of these people, while
absolving them of any responsibility for what I have
written. That responsibility is mine alone. I simply
hope that each can see his influence and will recognize
that whatever merit this work has I owe to my friends.

TABLE OF CONTENTS

CHAPTER 1
INTRODUCTION

St. Augustine is not usually numbered among the world's important epistemologists. This claim would seem odd to a writer in the late middle ages, for Augustine's philosophical successors engaged in extensive debate centered on his theory of illumination. However, Augustine's theory of knowledge is generally ignored by contemporary philosophers. There are several reasons for this. First, Augustine's obvious influence has been theological and political. Second, his epistemology is embedded in -- and is often concealed by -- other elements of his thought. Third, those who have written on Augustine's theory of knowledge have often simply repeated his metaphors without interpretation. Thus, we have his account explained by appeal to such notions as the inner-eye, vital attention and illumination -- the very notions that must themselves be explained. The fourth reason Augustine is ignored as an epistemologist is one of the central goals of this study. I will argue that Augustine's epistemology is, in many crucial respects, related to the Idealist tradition. Until recently, Idealism in its various forms has been held in disrepute. Recent trends have rendered Augustine's sort of Idealism tenable.

My motive in this analysis is to convince contemporary philosophers -- especially those who are

usually labeled as "analysts" -- that Augustine is an
important epistemologist. In order to achieve this end
I have set three goals for this study. My first task
is to demonstrate that there is a unified epistemology
contained, both explicitly and implicitly, in
Augustine's work. Some preliminary remarks will clarify the notion of a unified epistemology.

An epistemology ought to deal with several sorts
of factual knowledge: knowledge of the material world,
memory (knowledge of the past), and knowledge of general integrative principles (for present purposes we
may think of this as *a priori* or universal knowledge).
An epistemology must provide an account of how these
various sorts of knowledge are attained. This account
should include a coherent overview relating the various
sorts of knowledge and should also explain error.
Finally, an epistemology ought to provide an account of
personal knowledge, of the extent to which the putative
knower knows himself.

The ideal, then, is an epistemology that accomplishes these four broad tasks in an internally consistent, coherent, and open manner. Consistency and
coherence are notions that will be familiar to philosophers. By openness I mean versatility. A versatile
epistemology allows us to deal with new circumstances
and new epistemic situations. My first goal is to
demonstrate that Augustine's account of knowledge
meets these requirements.

My second goal is to present Augustine's epistemology without hiding behind the usual metaphors. For
example, in presenting his theory of perception commentators have often used the formula "the soul presides over the body by means of vital attention." In
my analysis of Augustine's account of our knowledge of
the material world I explain that metaphor. I also

explain Augustine's account of *a priori* knowledge --
his theory of illumination. I argue that Augustine
treats general ideas as mapping concepts. In meeting
my second goal a non-theistic epistemology emerges.
This is deliberate. Augustine is a theist. But he is
also a man who values the powers of human reason. The
human mind resembles God more closely than does any
other created thing. As a consequence of this resem-
blance it has the capacity to know. I demonstrate how
powerful Augustine took that capability to be.

My third goal is to characterize Augustine's epistemology generally and, consequently, to tie that epistemology to others in the history of philosophy. This
will require a detailed consideration of what has been
called Augustine's "interiority." Augustine makes extensive use of such phrases as "inner-man," "inner-
sight," and "inner-hearing." He uses these locutions
for many reasons, but one of the most important is his
recognition that coming to know involves the imposition
of a conceptual scheme upon the confusion of experience.
Knowledge, then, is a consequence of a process of clar-
ification. Fifteen centuries before the advent of
Linguistic Phenomenalism and the resurgence of Idealism,
Augustine recognized that the phenomena requiring epistemic explanation are essentially and irreducibly
inner, whether they concern an awareness of the apparent passage of time, our knowledge of material objects,
memory of the past, or our understanding of necessary
truths. In all of these cases the fundamental datum
is something true about the knower -- an inner phenomenon. Building on the foundation of these inner phenomena, Augustine constructs a conceptual scheme
providing a unified account of knowledge.

The present work, then, is a treatment of
Augustine's theory of knowledge which analyzes the

individual elements of that theory and relates those
elements into a unified structure. The analysis does
not involve a simple repetition of Augustine's modes of
explanation; in fact, central to this treatment of
Augustine is an account of his various explanatory
devices. The analysis ties Augustine to other epistemologists, especially to those in the Idealist tradition. In this the account is non-theistic, it is
focused on the role of reason, rather than that of
authority. This last point is, perhaps, the element in
my approach to Augustine that is most controversial.
It depends upon showing that Augustine's epistemology
is grounded in reason. (Or, less extremely, that
Augustine's epistemology may be understood in a purely
rational manner.) Although this claim will only be
established as a consequence of my extended argument, I
can make some preliminary remarks about it here.

Augustine maintains that, "What we know we hold in
the grasp of reason."[1] Reason has had many meanings in
the history of philosophy. To say that Augustine's
epistemology is rational is, I think, to say a number
of specific things. Most importantly, Augustine's
conceptual scheme is ordered schematically and ontologically; it exhibits structure and requires purpose.
The various aspects of that scheme must be unified both
conceptually (in that no element of the scheme can be
inconsistent with any other element of that scheme) and
teleologically (in that all elements play a role in the
development of a coherent view of the world).

To say that his account is rational is also to say
that the mind plays an active role in knowledge.
Augustine's is a creative view of knowledge. Knowledge
is not passively obtained from an external, objective
reality. Rather, the elements of knowledge are constructed by the mind. Thus, the mind is central to

Augustine's treatment of knowledge -- his position is dualistic.

Many contemporary philosophers are convinced that dualism is an inadequate account of human nature. I do not enter this debate, but I do think that the usual criticism of dualism borders on the precious. Augustine does not talk about a ghost in a machine. Rather, he introduces talk about minds in order to explain phenomena that would otherwise be unexplained. In addition, the approach he takes to his conceptual scheme is one that requires the existence of a mind and does not *require* anything else.

This last point bears expansion. One task of philosophy is the determination of the kinds of things that exist. This ontological enterprise is only important to the degree that the existing things may be related to human beings. These relationships may be drawn in several different ways, each way having ontological implications.

One way to treat existence is to begin with a multiplicity of independently existing things and then to relate those things to human beings. For example, one might begin with a world of material objects, relating that world to human experience by holding that some portion of that experience is caused by those material things. There are trees and rocks and there are human beings. The epistemological task becomes one of relating human beings to material objects.

Another way to treat existence is to begin with the raw data for any conceptual scheme -- human experience -- and then to construct a picture of reality on the basis of such data. In this sort of schema I know that I have many kinds of experiences. The epistemological task is to understand and explain these experiences. Most often, such explanations have

ontological consequences. If the world is constituted
in a particular way, then I will have experiences of a
particular sort.

Augustine takes the latter approach. His account
has an ontologically simple first state, although the
resultant conceptual scheme is ontologically complex.
The complexity, however, emerges as the rational explanation of experience develops; it is not a characteristic of Augustine's starting point.

In part, the complexity of Augustine's conceptual
scheme is a consequence of a common Augustinian device.
He will frequently consider several possible explanations for a particular phenomenon. Eventually, the
explanations best suited to the puzzling data emerge.
The explanations that finally prove acceptable will be
those that cover the broadest range -- usually, these
will be the most complex.

Augustine's epistemology may be complex, but it is
also holistic; it is a view composed of individual elements that are tied to each other in crucial ways. In
a sense, this requires some understanding of all of
Augustine's epistemology before any individual compo-
nent of it may be understood. As a consequence, it is
difficult to know where to begin this exposition. My
solution to this problem is to deal first with
Augustine's means of explanation. When he explains
knowledge he writes of an inner-man whose inner-eye
perceives certain kinds of objects. We now turn our
attention to this means of explanation. After clarifying his explanatory devices, it will be easier to
deal with the various elements of his epistemology.

Chapter 1

Footnote

[1] *Quidquid enim scimus, id ratione comprehensum tenemus.* *De Libero Arbitrio* (hereafter DLA) II, 3, 9. A complete chart of the abbreviations used in this book begins on page 228.

CHAPTER 2
THE INNER MAN

Augustine's explanatory device

Most writers who consider Augustine comment on his "interiority." Augustine writes of an inner-man, inner-sight, inner-speech and inner-hearing. Despite the pervasiveness of these inner-man locutions, no one has tried to provide an extended analysis of his use of this language. It is supposed to be evidence for meta-physical dualism. I do not deny that Augustine is a dualist, but there is more to his use of inner-man locutions. Such locutions are devices that make his dualism plausible and coherent. Writing of the mind as *homo interior* may eventually lead Augustine into diffi-culties, but those difficulties are not obvious ones.

Augustine uses the inner-man locutions in two important ways. First, he uses them to explain various aspects of his epistemology. Second, he uses them to explain how we judge and report on our judgments. In this section I outline the various uses that Augustine has for his inner-man locutions. I also consider the chronological development of his use of those locutions, and present a theory about the sort of explanatory device they constitute. In the concluding chapter I shall return to the inner-man and evaluate its useful-ness as an explanatory device.

I

Explanation by means of analogy is common,
especially when the explanandum is mysterious or escapes
direct observation. For example, a physics teacher
might explain a nuclear reaction by using mouse traps
and ping pong balls. When Augustine explains how we
know -- especially when he explains *a priori* knowledge
-- he writes of inner-lights, inner eyes, and inner-
men. Augustine's use of inner-man locutions shares
important characteristics with a physics teacher's use
of mouse traps and ping pong balls -- in Augustine's
account of knowledge the inner-man locutions have a
theoretical and methodological role similar to that of
analogue models in scientific explanations.

Augustine recognizes that knowledge is a complicated process which involves more than a simple confrontation with the world. He values inner-man
locutions for their utility in explaining that process,
especially in the context of his theory of illumination.
Augustine's theory of illumination, which I shall discuss in Chapter 6, is an analysis of knowledge of
eternal truths (knowledge that more recent philosophers
would characterize as *a priori*). Augustine's suggestion is that a man's physical domain shares a calculus
with a man's mental domain. To say that two domains
share a calculus is to say that, in certain crucial
respects, they share a logical structure; that there
are ways of talking that may be appropriately applied
to both domains. For Augustine a man's body and its
environment share a calculus with a man's mind and its
environment. His vehicle for explicating this shared
calculus is the inner-man locution.

It is not my purpose either to defend or to excuse
metaphysical dualism, only to show that Augustine gives
an impressive account of it -- an account that explains

knowledge that he found inconceivable to deny (knowledge
of God) and knowledge that even contemporary philosophers find difficult to explain (knowledge of analytic
truths and logical principles). Whether or not metaphysical dualism adequately characterizes human nature,
Augustine's version is not the simple mistake of the
ghost in the machine.

II

Chronology of the Inner Man

Treating the mind as a human being within the human
body is not uncommon. Augustine's use of inner-man
locutions, however, is extraordinarily extensive and
sophisticated. My primary task here is to consider the
historical development of inner-man locutions in
Augustine's works. The examination takes two
approaches. First, I consider the chronology of inner-
man locutions in his earlier works, determining when,
and in what contexts, Augustine began to use such locutions. Second, there are early works of Augustine's in
which inner-man locutions either do not occur at all or
are quite primitive where they do occur. For these
earlier works I have considered Augustine's comments in
his *Retractiones* about certain key passages. The passages I am interested in are those which deal with
problems that would have called for the use of inner-
man locutions, had the works been written later in
Augustine's career. Of course, Augustine does not
write, "Here I should have used inner-man locutions."
However, Augustine does make it fairly clear in his
comments on earlier works (especially *Contra Academicos*)
that in the Cassiciacum period he was not thinking
along the inner-outer lines that so characterize his
later work. Inner-man locutions occur more frequently
as his epistemological views become more sophisticated.

This increasing frequency is due to his recognition of the utility of inner-man talk.

The dialogues reported in *Contra Academicos* probably occurred on November 10-11 and 20-22 in 386 in Cassiciacum.[2] Augustine indicates in *Retractiones*[3] that two of his early works, *De Ordine* and *De Beata Vita*, were written after Book I and before Book III of *Contra Academicos*. Thus, we have three works that represent Augustine's style early in his literary career.

In *Contra Academicos* Augustine replies to the sceptical claim that there is no certain knowledge, that all knowledge is grounded on probability. Regarding the certainty of knowledge, Augustine maintains that truth can be derived from "...the combined weight of authority and reason."[4] He adheres to this view throughout his life. He also anticipates his doctrine of illumination in asserting that truth can only be gained by one who maintains a hold on the "...knots of comprehension,"[5] and by taking God's mind as the repository of his equivalent of Plato's forms.[6] He does not use inner-man locutions.[7] In fact, in a context in which, in later works, Augustine would have appealed to inner-man locutions, he does not.

> Who would doubt that there is nothing
> better in a man than that part of the
> soul which properly dominates all other
> things in a man and to which all other
> things should submit as to their ruler?
> However, unless you insist on another
> definition, this can be called the mind
> or reason.[8]

In later works the ruler of a man is said to be his heart or the inner-man or the inner-teacher, and Augustine will use inner-man locutions to *demonstrate how* the inner-man is the ruler of the body.

In *Retractiones* Augustine seems to have recognized
that there were passages in *Contra Academicos* which
appear ambiguous when considered in light of his later
work

> Concerning that section in which I said,
> "Nothing among all which the bodily eye
> can see or any of the senses can discern
> should be valued and all should be de-
> spised," words should be added so that
> it says, "whatever a sense of the mortal
> body discerns, for there is also the
> mind's sense." But *then* I was talking
> as those who apply "sense" only to the
> body, and "sensible" only to material
> things. (Italics added)[9]

He recognizes that at the time of writing *Contra
Academicos* he used such words as "sense" ambiguously,
not keeping clear the distinction between the special
inner senses and the outer senses.

In *De Beata Vita* Augustine argues that happiness
may be gained only through truth, which he identifies
with God. He uses a primitive inner-man locution.
"There is...a real sterility and hunger of the soul.
Just as the body is generally ill and mangy when nutri-
tion is withheld...so is the impoverishment of souls
shown by illness..."[10]   He does not do much with this
metaphor beyond showing that there are "...two kinds of
food for souls: one good...the other bad."[11]
Augustine does not discuss soul food later. Neverthe-
less, this is an instructive case, since he here uses
a common physical experience to demonstrate a point
about a non-physical state (although, of course, he
does not speak here of the soul's being inner).

Later in *De Beata Vita* there is a more forceful
use of an inner-man locution. We are urged

> ...to remember God and to search for him
> and to thirst after the fountain of truth...
> That secret sun pours that splendid light
> into our innermost place. His truth is all
> the truth which we speak, despite our hesi-
> tation, in our anxiety, to turn bravely
> toward this light and to regard it fully,
> because *our eyes*, only recently opened,
> are not strong enough yet. This light
> seems to be God...(Italics added)[12]

This passage is important for several reasons.
Augustine speaks of eyes which are not yet strong
enough to fully regard something illuminated by an inner
sun. He is not writing about bodily eyes but of a kind
of inner eye. His discussion of such eyes in this context, which treats God as the source of truth and as
the proper guide to life, indicates that even at this
early stage he used a kind of inner-man locution to ex-
hort his reader to seek truth. His writing about understanding (or knowledge) in terms of a light shining
within is also important. This is an early mention of
the doctrine of illumination, and there is reason to
believe that Augustine was not aware of the significance
of the passage at the time of its writing, for one month
later he wrote that eternal truths are drawn from ob-
livion or dug out by the mind,[13] assuming a view very
much like Platonic reminiscence. Later Augustine will
deny Platonic reminiscence in favor of illumination, an
account of *a priori* knowledge more consonant with inner-
lights and inner-eyes. There is one final significance
to the passage from *De Beata Vita*. By locating truth
in the mind of God, Augustine sets the stage for his
important view that epistemology and morals are closely
tied.

Augustine does not make further points with inner-
man locutions in this passage. Mention of a secret sun

and (inner) eyes occurs at the culmination of a
discussion of goodness as the proper object of human
pursuit, *after* the discussion has been concluded. In
Augustine's more mature work he is more likely to use
inner-man locutions to *explicate* his view rather than
stating it in other terms first and then using the
inner-man talk as a sort of rhetorical frosting.

The third of his early dialogues is *De Ordine*,
which considers the problem of evil. It, too, was
written during the winter of 386 in Cassiciacum as a
literary farewell to Manichaeism. *De Ordine*, more than
any of the earlier dialogues, hints at the central elements of Augustine's more mature philosophy.

For my present purpose, the most important section
of *De Ordine* begins at Book II, 11,30. Augustine has
just completed a long and somewhat opaque dissertation
in the importance of authority for knowledge. He now
begins to discuss reason, the second important element
in knowing. He admits, however, that "...although men
try to act completely rationally when dealing with
those things most likely to deceive, only a few know
what reason is or what its properties are."[14] He suggests that there is a convenient way to understand
reason, however, "...to the degree that reason has allowed itself to be shown in things that are familiar to
you let us investigate it as well as we can..."[15] This
is not, of course, an inner-man locution. However, the
program suggested is the program on which the inner-man
locutions are based -- the attempt to understand something mysterious or peculiar (in this case, the processes of reasoning) through appeal to something
common and readily available (the kinds of things one
is familiar with).

In *Retractiones* we see that Augustine makes only
one positive remark about *De Ordine*, and that remark
concerns the method suggested above.

> This subject is a difficult one to
> understand. When I realized that it
> could not be understood without dis-
> pute by those with whom I was dealing
> I preferred to talk about a way of
> studying through which we could advance
> from the physical to the incorporeal.[16]

As to explicit inner-man locutions, the pickings
are slim. In discussing beauty, Augustine tells us that
reason seeks a beauty which would be accessible only to
reason and from which reason would not be distracted by
physical sensation. "Therefore, its gaze turned
slightly toward the senses."[17] The metaphor does not
play a role in his following discussion of the particular senses and the ways in which each sense's peculiar
objects may or may not be beautiful. This seems to be
the only inner-man locution of significance in *De
Ordine*.

The last work Augustine gives us from the
Cassiciacum period is *Soliloquia*. In *Retractiones* he
describes the first book of *Soliloquia* as being concerned to investigate "...what a man ought to be like
who wishes to embrace wisdom, which is grasped not by a
bodily sense but by the mind..."[18] In dealing with
this problem Augustine uses inner-man locutions in ways
similar to the ways they are used in his later works.
Here Augustine begins to describe what permits man to
have knowledge *a priori*.

> Reason speaks to you and promises to
> allow you to see God with your mind in
> the way that the sun is seen with the
> eye. The mind has, as it were, its own
> eyes. The certain truths of knowledge
> are something like objects which are
> made visible by the sun...[19]

In one of his earliest works, then, Augustine makes
use of an important inner-man locution -- "the eye of
the mind." Two things are significant in his usage of
"mind's eye" in these earlier dialogues: first, it is
metaphorical and literary, prefixed by *quasi*; second, it
is "mind's eye" rather than "inner-vision" or "sight of
the inner-man," As yet, Augustine has not mentioned
homo interior.

In *De Immortalitate Animae*, written in 387, and in
De Quantitate Animae, written in 388, Augustine continues to be concerned with the problem of *a priori*
knowledge. "Those things that are understood by the
intellect...are understood as existing in the mind
itself..."[20] In order to account for our access to
things comprehended by the intellect Augustine appeals
to an inner faculty. Now, however, he does not speak
of an inner-eye but of inner-sight. "Reason is the
sight of the mind through which it grasps truth without
the help of the body..."[21] Again, at *De Quantitate
Animae* he tells us that

> ...when the mind's sight, which we call
> reason, sees something, we call that
> knowledge. But when the mind does not
> see, even though it focuses its sight,
> that is called not-knowing or ignorance.[22]

This shift from inner-eye talk to inner-sight talk is
important. Up to this point Augustine is concerned to
explicate knowledge of necessary truth, but his explication has been restricted to talk about a Divine Mind
or Divine Ideas. He seems to have realized at about
this time, however, that his account of knowledge *a
priori* must appeal to an irreducibly inner state. By
placing the objects of such knowledge (whatever they
may be) within, it becomes necessary for him to use
inner-man locutions to explicate our access to them.

It is difficult to exactly date Augustine's first
explicit use of *homo interior*. It is either in a passage from *De Genesi Contra Manichaeos*, written between
388 and 390, or in a passage from *De Magistro*, written
in 389. The passage from *De Genesi Contra Manichaeos*
appears in the context of a discussion of the claim
that man is made in God's image. "...it is said that
man is made in God's image, this is said after (about)
the inner-man, where reason and intellect are..."[23]
The more certainly datable *De Magistro* is a report of a
conversation which occurred between Augustine and his
son, Adeodatus. It deals with Augustine's developing
epistemology and reveals the extent to which Augustine's
developing view of knowledge required more frequent use
of special inner facilities and objects. He begins the
discussion by again treating the problem of our access
to God, and thus, to *a priori* knowledge. "...God should
be sought in the secret places of the rational soul,
which is called the inner-man..."[24] A new inner-man
locution emerges in *De Magistro*, "inner-speech," a
notion which is important for his treatment of deliberate action and communication. "...even when we do not
utter a sound, because we think words, we speak with
the mind..."[25] This "speaking within the mind" occurs
in a discussion of a relationship between man and God,
in this case showing why there is no need to speak
aloud during prayer.

In *De Vera Religione* (389-391) Augustine continues
to tie inner-man locutions to his epistemology, "Truth
lives in the inner-man."[26] Until 394 and *De Mendacio*
the inner-man locutions concentrate on an explanation
of knowledge of eternal truths and are restricted to
two basic forms, "inner-man" and "inner-sight" (this
latter being modified slightly in *De Sermone Domini in
Monte* to include "sight of the heart" as in "...he

would see God with the heart...")[27]   In *De Mendacio*,
however, Augustine considers lying, and in considering
lying he adds a further inner-man locution: "the inner-
mouth" or "mouth of the heart." He credits Scripture
with this usage. "Often when Scripture says 'mouth' it
means the inner chamber of the heart..."[28]   Again, a
relationship between God and Man is explicated by inner-
man locutions, for God knows when someone is lying because He can hear the words uttered by the inner-mouth.

     This theme of the inner-mouth's being the source
of sin is continued in *De Continentia* written at about
the same time as *De Mendacio*.

> Many things are done by men with closed
> mouth, quiet tongue, stilled voice, but
> nothing is done by the body that is not
> first said in the heart. So, because
> there are many sins in inner-words which
> are not expressed in outer actions...
> innocence will be from both.[29]

Inner-man talk is here being used to explain human
action, but *primarily* because a rationale is needed for
punishment of intentions.

     In *Confessiones*, written eleven years after *Contra
Academicos*, Augustine uses inner-man locutions to express the dual nature of man. "Now, there is obviously
a body and a soul in me, one exterior and one interi-
or."[30]   By the time of *Confessiones*, then, Augustine
has developed the inner-man locutions from a metaphor
which is handy as a kind of rhetorical dividend, to a
set of metaphors, including the two most important of
the inner-man locutions, "inner-sight" and "inner-
speech." Having developed the metaphors to this degree,
he uses them in treating all aspects of his epistemology. Sometimes his use of these locutions is straight-
forward, as in *De Trinitate*, "What...a physical object

is to the bodily sense, an image is to the eye of the
mind."[31]   Other times, as in the three-fold theory of
vision presented in *De Genesi ad Litteram*, he uses them
subtly. Whether used subtly or straightforwardly, the
inner-man metaphor dominates Augustine's explication of
knowledge. Having traced the chronological development
of that metaphor, I shall now discuss the inner/outer
distinction itself.

III

Augustine believes that there are two realms in the universe. One is the familiar realm of material objects.
The other is a spiritual, mental realm. His intellectual development may be seen as a series of flirtations
with attempts to relate these realms. He began with
Manichaeism, which radicalizes the dichotomy, treating
the material realm as the haven of goodness. He soon
recognized the poverty of this view, and came to embrace
neo-Platonism, a more rational position that offers
argument in place of harangue and philosophy in place
of mysticism. Further, neo-Platonism does not treat
the world as being essentially evil. In fact, it
treats the body as a useful tool for dealing with the
material world, recognizing as well that sometimes the
material world interferes with the soul's desire to do
good.

The ultimate product of Augustine's search is a
Christianity that utilizes neo-Platonism. His account
of the relationship between the spiritual and the corporeal realms is influenced by both St. Paul and such
neo-Platonists as Plotinus and Cicero. The two realms
are united in human beings, whom Augustine treats as
having an inner and an outer aspect. In contrast to
the view that Augustine's interiority is evidence for
metaphysical dualism, I shall argue that his division
of human nature into inner and outer characteristics is

an explanatory device; it is not intended to be de-
descriptive. Another way to put this point is to say
that his discussion of a difficulty in one place by
using inner-man locutions does not rule out his explaining the same subject in another place by using
outer-man locutions in a different way. This will be
especially clear in his analysis of perception. Since
his use of the inner/outer dichotomy is so flexible,
it is important at the outset to clarify the distinction between the inner and the outer man.

The Outer Man

     At *De Trinitate* XII, I,1 Augustine asserts that the
outer man is not just the body; it also includes all of
those qualities and abilities which human beings share
with other animals. The outer man includes the body,
the body's senses, and all of the conditions which must
be fulfilled in order to keep the body alive. This
last task of the outer man requires some explanation,
as Augustine seems to contradict himself. In *De
Trinitate* the outer man gives life to the body.[32] In
Confessiones it is the soul that does this.[33] In both
places he uses the word *vita*.

     The best way around this difficulty is to take as
outer all that keeps the body alive and functioning,
while taking as inner that which gives a man, as a combination of soul and body, his vitality. An example
should prove helpful.

     Imagine a man who is kept alive by various ma-
chines which stimulate his organs to keep them functioning; machines that keep his heart beating and his
lungs breathing and his kidneys filtering. Suppose
that a body, connected to such machinery, registers a
flat brain-tracing on an EEG read-out. Even in the
absence of brain-activity, the body could be kept

functioning, at least for a time. To add a bit of
science fiction, one can imagine the body as being
transplanted to a new brain and coming to function more
or less normally. Whatever these machines do to keep a
body functioning is an activity performed by the outer-
man in the case of a healthy person. The soul provides
a human being with his vitality; the outer-man provides
the body with all that it needs to stay alive. There
are various conditions that must be fulfilled in order
for a body to function. The outer-man provides these
conditions; the inner-man uses the body, directing the
application of its various functions and abilities.
Since Augustine identifies a man with his soul, the
seeming contradiction is erased, the body keeps itself
alive, the soul keeps the man alive.

The outer-man also includes the five bodily senses,
which are used for the perception of material objects.
When the body's senses perceive something material, a
"message" is sent to the mind where an image is generated. This image is stored in the memory, and when we
remember the particular material objects this image is
recalled. Such recollection is "...still a thing per-
taining to the outer-man."[34]

The function of the outer-man is fairly straight-
forward: It is used by the soul. A human being is
"...a rational soul having (or using) a body..."[35]
The outer-man has two major uses. He is responsible
for the perception of corporeal things, his senses
sending messages to the mind, and he provides the
means *via* which one inner-man may communicate something to another.

The inner-Man

For Augustine the inner-man is the mind.
"...{D}escend into yourself, go to your secret place,
your mind..."[36] He tells us in *De Trinitate* (X,7,9)

that some philosophers suppose that the mind or the soul
is a part of the body, and they wonder just which part
of the body it is. Augustine does not write of the mind
as being spatially inner. The mind is not "...within,
as if in your body..."[37] as a lung or some other organ
is within the body, nor is the mind a part of the body
as a hand or a foot is a part of the body. Rather, the
mind is in the body in the way that health is in the
body or age is in the body. Having a mind is true of
human bodies, although a mind is not a part of a body
any more than health is a part of a body.

The importance of man as the ontological joining
of the material and spiritual worlds can be seen in
Augustine's forceful admonishment:

> Return to your heart, see there whatever
> it may be that you sense of God, for in
> it is the image of God. Christ dwells
> in the inner man, in the inner-man you
> are renewed after the image of God, in[38]
> His image recognize its Author.

The claim that man is in God's image is a controversial
one. A common patristic view is that man was origi-
nally created in God's image and likeness, but after
the fall he lost His likeness but not His image.
Augustine rejected this view on purely philosophical
grounds. He maintains that if x is an image of y there
must be in x some likeness to y; it would be impossible
for x to image y if a likeness of some sort were
absent.[39]   Thus, in discussing the nature of God
Augustine writes:

> ...I do not travel very far for examples
> when I mean to give you some similitude
> to your God from your own mind, for cer-
> tainly not in the body, but in the same[40]
> mind, was man made after the image of God.

It is man's mind which is in God's image. The image may
be perfected (or "renewed"), or it may be distorted
through sin, but the image remains.

Augustine draws a parallel between the inner-man's
imaging God and the outer-man's imaging the inner-man.
In order to count as the mind of a man the mind must be
an image of God. It is not that a mind was created
first and was then given the quality of being in God's
image. Rather, if the inner-man were not in God's
image in the first place, the concatenation of inner
and outer-man would not be called a man. Of course, the
outer-man is also called "man." "For that (outer-man)
is not called man for no reason, but because there is
in him some similarity to the inner-man."[41] For
Augustine it is not a mistake to call the outer-man
"man" because the outer-man is created in the inner-
man's image.

Augustine sometimes writes of the inner-man as
being a man's heart.[42] He does not mean literally the
physical heart. "...{Y}our body is not what your heart
is; leave even your body, return to your heart."[43] In
De Continentia Augustine offers an interpretation of
Matthew 15:8: "The things that proceed out of the
mouth, come from the heart."

> ...it is just as though He said, "When
> you hear from the mouth, understand
> from the heart." I say both, but I use
> one to expound the other. The inner
> man has an inner-mouth, and an inner-
> ear discerns this.[44]

He also indicates that "...{H}e who praises in his
heart praises with the voice of the inner-man..."[45]

The inner-man is able to see, hear, taste, touch
and smell. At *In Johannis Evangelium XCIX, 2-4*,
Augustine discusses the sort of knowledge that God may

have. He maintains that God has sight, hearing, taste,
touch and smell (he offers appropriate passages of
Scripture for each), but he warns that he does not mean
to imply that God has sense organs scattered throughout
His body. It might seem peculiar to express the sort of
ineffable wisdom that God has in terms of bodily senses,
but Augustine points out that we do this when we speak
of (another non-corporeal thing) the mind:

> ...even our own mind, in other words,
> the inner man...is said both to see
> the light, of which it is said, "That
> was the true light"; and to hear the
> word, of which it is said, "In the be-
> ginning was the word"; and to be sus-
> ceptible to smell, of which it is said,
> "We will run after the smell of your
> ointments"; and to drink of the fountain,
> of which it is said, "With you is the
> fountain of life"; and to enjoy the
> sense of touch, of which it is said,
> "But it is good for me to cleave unto
> God..."[46]

Two things are clear from this passage: The inner-man
has senses, and the objects of these senses are not
corporeal things; they are spiritual. Before considering the inner-man's senses, the nature of the objects of his senses, and how the two are related, an
important question must be considered: Does the inner-
man have non-material sense organs? The question is
important because the notion that the inner-man has
diverse and distinct senses (and, thus, diverse and
distinct sense organs) is essential to the view that
the inner/outer dichotomy is descriptive rather than
explanatory. There is some evidence in support of the
view that the inner-man does have such senses, for

example, the passage quoted immediately above. There
are other references to inner senses, almost exclusively referring to inner-sight and inner-hearing.
Augustine supports the view that the heart has ears and
eyes through appeal to Scripture. If the inner-man
does not have ears, he asks, then why does Luke have
the Lord say, "Who so hath ears to hear let him hear."
And why did Paul say, "The eyes of your heart being
enlightened,"[47] if the heart has no eyes? There is a
mouth of the heart as well: "In one sentence he has
encompassed the diverse mouths of man, the one bodily,
the other of the heart."[48] And, the inner-ear hears
this mouth: "The inner-man has an inner-mouth and an
inner-ear hears this."[49]

These passages may lead one to the view that
Augustine's picture of the inner-man is literally one
of an actual, non-material man who has real senses and
sense-organs. But we may well ask whether the analogy
is intended to be so strict.

Augustine asks, "In your body you find eyes in one
place, ears in another place; do you find this in your
heart?"[50] God's senses are not distributed throughout
His body. "...{I}n that substantiality which is God
the senses are not distributed in their appropriate
places, as if through some material structure of a
body..."[51] Since the inner-man is created in God's
image, it is not surprising for Augustine to say,
"Show me the eyes, ears, nostrils of your heart. The
things that are referred to the heart are diverse, but
there are not diverse organs there."[52] Whatever does
the heart's seeing and hearing is apparently one thing.
"In your flesh you hear in one place, see in another;
in your heart, where you see, there you hear."[53]

However, showing that the inner-man does not have
a diversity of inner, non-material sense organs does

not rule out the inner-man's having a diversity of
sense functions. He may still smell and taste and hear.
A strictly literal interpretation of inner-man locutions
continues to be a live possibility. In order to elimi-
nate this possibility I shall establish that for
Augustine inner-seeing, hearing, and so on, are really
different ways of speaking of the same thing.

> For God, all of the senses are apparently the same.
> Both to see and to hear exist together
> in the word. Seeing and hearing are
> not diverse things in Him, but hearing
> is sight and sight is hearing.[54]

Now, Augustine has given us scriptural support for God's
having sight, hearing, smell, taste, and touch. When
God is said to know "...all are included: seeing and
hearing, smelling and tasting, and touching..."[55]
There are two things to be noted about this passage.
First, Augustine is not saying that God knows a seeable
thing by seeing it, a hearable thing by hearing it, and
so on. When anything is known, it is known by all of
His senses. Secondly, it may seem peculiar that one
would express the sort of eternal knowledge that God
has by writing of Him as though He had a body. However, as I noted earlier, Augustine points out that
this is not all that unusual, since we do something
like this whenever we write or speak of our own minds.

This analogy between God-talk and mind-talk may
be advanced further. It is important to note here that
the dominant case for Augustine's epistemology and his
use of inner-man locutions -- knowledge of principal
ideas *via* illumination -- is a special kind of relationship that man's mind has to the mind of God. This
adds to the significance of our discussion of the similarity between God-talk and mind-talk.

In *De Trinitate* we see that for the mind (as for
God) seeing and hearing are the same thing.

> For when these things are done outwardly
> by means of the body, then speech and
> sight are different things. But, when
> we think inwardly the two are one. Just
> as sight and hearing are two things
> mutually distinct in the bodily senses,
> but to see and hear are the same thing
> in the mind. And thus, while speech is
> not seen but rather heard outwardly,
> yet the same inward speeches, that is,
> thoughts, are seen in the Holy Gospel
> to have been seen, and not heard, by the
> Lord.[56]

So, it is not just that the mind sees and hears at the
same place, but seeing and hearing are the same sort of
apprehension for the inner-man.

This is made explicit by Augustine in *In Johannis
Evangelium*. He has admitted that talk about God's
knowledge in terms usually reserved for bodily or
material things seems unusual, but he supports such
talk by pointing out that we speak of our own minds as
though they saw, heard, and so on. He warns, however,
that it is a mistake to think that we are speaking of
diverse senses when we talk this way, for "...it is not
different things, but the one intelligence, that is expressed by the names of so many senses."[57]

One striking characteristic of the passages cited
above, and of Augustine's use of the inner-man in general, is that the senses that are characterized as
"different ways of speaking of the same thing," etc.,
are primarily inner-sight and inner-hearing. As we
shall see, for Augustine the sight of the mind and
inner-words are intimately connected.

Augustine does not hold that the inner-man has
either diverse sense organs or diverse senses. When he

writes of inner-vision, inner-hearing, etc. he is
writing about the same thing, the process of knowing.

However, Augustine often writes of the inner-eye,
the inner-ear, the mouth of the heart. Showing what he
does *not* mean by these locutions rules out only a very
primitive and unsympathetic interpretation. One still
must explain why he uses these ways of speaking.

IV

Augustine employs inner-man locutions with increasing frequency, and he depends upon them to explain
certain of his epistemological views, because he recognizes that inner-man locutions have a high degree of
explanatory power. He is aware of a way of explanation
which is very much like the device of analogue modeling
used in science. In order to demonstrate the utility
of inner-man talk I shall now consider some important
characteristics of such modeling.[58]
Analogue Models and Explanation

Natural phenomena that appear mysterious may often
be clarified and explained through analogies. The ef-
fectiveness of such explanation depends upon analogical
similarities between the domain of the explanans and
the domain of the explanandum. The appropriate similarities might be among physical behaviors, as when the
behavior of a gas in a container is explained by
talking about billiard balls on a billiard table. On
the other hand, these similarities might also consist
in the fact that the explanans and the explanandum
follow similar rules. For example, economic phenomena,
such as the relationship between supply and demand, may
be explained by talking about the behavior of a pair of
cylinders in a closed hydraulic system. The internal
properties and interrelationships of each system constitute a calculus. The similarities holding between
the domain of the explanans and that of the explanandum
may be seen as reflecting a shared calculus.

The suggestion made in analogical explanation is that notions appropriate to the domain of the explanans may be used to help understand the explanandum, even when the explanans is a material object and the explanandum is a complex social interaction (as when we are told to think of the economy as a hydraulic system). Appropriateness is measured by the degree to which a calculus is shared.

Analogue models are powerful kinds of analogies that serve more than rhetorical and pedagogical purposes. Through extension, analogue models can often advance our knowledge of prototypes. (For example, by treating gases as though they consisted of elastic spheres in constant motion we can learn new things about gases.)

In general, a model is a representation of its prototype which exhibits crucial properties of the prototype in a more readily available medium. It is the representation of these crucial properties that makes models important. Facts learned about models may be facts learned about prototypes in certain cases, where these cases are determined by whatever properties or relationships the model exhibits that are (or would be) exhibited by the prototype (i.e., cases in which the model and the prototype share a calculus). Unlike systems that are constructed to serve as models, analogue models are chosen from among existing systems or objects and analogies are then drawn between prototype and model.

The use of an analogue model is especially important when the prototype is not empirically examinable. In such cases a model can often advance our understanding, since every model exhibits characteristics that are not shared by the prototype. Such surplus meaning can be a dividend, in that the properties and

relationships of the model often help to predict and/or
explain properties hitherto unknown in the prototype.
However, a failure to recognize genuine disanalogies
can lead to serious problems, for one might instantiate
qualities in the prototype which are present only in
the model. Thus, an especially rich model can distort
rather than enhance understanding. Imagine someone's
replying to Plato's cave parable by asking, "Wouldn't
the smoke from the torches get into the cave-dweller's
eyes?"

In light of this danger, how do we determine
whether a model is a good one? I shall consider two
sorts of criteria for evaluating models. First, present
tense criteria, criteria which may be applied to a model
as it is selected. Second, past tense criteria, criteria which may be applied to a model after it has been
used.

Present Tense Criteria: A model is not advanced
in a vacuum, it is suggested for specific reasons. For
example, the prototype may be inaccessible to direct
observation, or the prototype may have certain properties that appear mysterious. In such cases it is helpful to consider a more readily available object,
drawing a set of analogies between that object and the
prototype which give the object analogue model status.
Several important factors are considered in selecting
the more readily available object, including the
nature of the audience, the properties of the prototype
that require explanation, whether the model carries
distorting surplus meaning (surplus meaning that cannot be readily isolated, "You don't need hydraulic
fluid in order to study economics."), the explainer's
preliminary assumptions about the prototype (the explainer may have a definite theoretical structure to
explain or he may have only a "likely story.")

Past Tense Criteria: There are other questions that may be asked once an analogue model has been selected.   If a model is *needed*, it must be because the prototype has properties or exhibits relationships that are puzzling.   Does the model solve these puzzles or clarify these relationships?   Does the model *extend* our understanding of the prototype?   In light of the provisional reasons for advancing the model, should the model be retained?   Is there an alternative model that would do a better job?

Augustine's famed "interiority" is more than a literary device.   An analogue model is a sophisticated means of explanation, one that must be consciously and carefully applied.   As we consider Augustine's epistemology I shall note the various ways that he uses inner-man locutions.   My hypothesis about the nature of these locutions will be supported by the degree to which they enhance Augustine's explanation of knowledge.   In the last chapter I shall return to an explicit consideration of the inner-man -- to an evaluation of the inner-man locutions as an explanatory device.

Chapter 2

Footnotes

[1]Gareth B. Matthews, "The Inner-Man," *American Philosophical Quarterly*, April 1967.

[2] D. Ohlman, *De Sancti Augustini dialogis in Cassiciaco Scriptis*, ("Der Elsasser" printing press, 1897), p. 27.

[3] *Retractiones* (hereafter RE), I, 2, 1.

[4] *Nulli autem dubium est germino pondere nos impelli as discendum, auctoritatis atque rationis. Contra Academicos* (hereafter CA) III, 20, 43.

[5] *...comprehensionis nodos...* CA III, 6, 13.

[6] CA III, 19, 42.

[7] He does tell us that God sent "...the authority of divine intellect down to the human body, and caused it to live within..." *...nisi summus Deus populari quadam clementia divini intellectus auctoritatem usque ad ipsum corpus humanum declinaret atque summitteret...* CA III, 19, 42.

[8]*Quis, inquam, dubitaverit, nihil aliud esse hominis optimum, quam eam partem animi, cui dominanti obtemperare convenit caetra quaeque in homine sunt? Haec autem, ne aliam postules definitionem, mens aut ratio dici potest.* CA I, 2, 5.

[9] *Itemque illic quod dixi, Nihil omnino colendum esse, totumque abjiciendum quidquid mortalibus oculis cernitur, quidquid ullus sensus attingit; addenda erant verba, ut diceretur quidquid mortalis corporis ullus sensus attingit: est enim sensus et mentis. Sed eorum more tunc loquebar, qui sensum non nisi corposis dicunt, et sensibilia non nisi corporalia. RE I, 1, 2.*

[10]
Ista ipsa est, inquam, crede mihi, quaedam sterilitas et quasi fames animorum. Nam quemadnodum corpus detracto cibo plerumque morbis atque scabie repletur, quae in eo vitia indicant famen; ita et illorum animi pleni sunt morbis quibus sua jejunia confitentur. De Beata Vita (hereafter DBV), 2, 8.

[11]*...ita animorum duo alimentorum genera inveniuntur; unum salubre atque utile, alterum morbidum atque pestiferum.* DBV, 2, 8.

[12]
Admonitio autem quaedam quae nobiscum agit, ut Deum recordemur, ut eum quaeramus, ut eum pulso omni fastidio sitiamus, de ipso ad nos fonte veritatis emanat. Hoc interioribus luminibus nostris jubar sol ille secretus infundit. Hujus est verum omne quod loquimur, etiam quando adhuc vel minus sanis vel repente apertis oculis audacter converti, et totum intueri trepidamus: nihilque aliud etiam hoc apparet esse quam Deum... DBV, 4, 35.

[13]
Soliloquia (hereafter SO) II, 20, 35.

[14]
...cum in rebus ipsis fallacibus ratione tytum agere homines moliantur, quid sit ipsa ratio, et qualis sit, nisi perpauci prorsus ignorant. De Ordine (hereafter DO) II, 11, 30.

[15]
Tamen quantum dignata est in res quae nobis notae videntur procedere, indagemus eam, si possumus interim... DO II, 11, 30.

[16]
Sed cum rem viderem ad intelligendum difficilem, satis aegre ad eorum perceptionem, cum quibus agebam, disputando posse perduci; de ordine studendi loqui malui, quo a corporalibus as incorporalia potest profici. RE I, 3, 1.

[17]
Itaque in eos ipsos paululum aciem torsit... DO II, 14, 39.

[18] *...qualis esse debeat qui vult percipere sapientiam quae utique non sensu corporis, sed mente percipitur.* RE I, 4, 1.

[19] *Promittit enium ratio quae tecum loquitur, ita se demonstraturam Deum tuae menti, ut oculis sol demonstratur. Nam mentis quasi sui sunt oculis sensus animae; disciplinarum autem quaeque certissima talia sunt, qualia illa quae sole illustrantur, ut videri possint...* SO I, 6, 12.

[20] *Ea vero quae intelliguntur, non quasi alibi posita intelliguntur, quam ipse qui intelligit animus. De Immortalitate Animae* (hereafter DIA) VI, 10.

[21] *Ratio est aspectus animi, quo per seipsum, non per corpus verum intuetur...* DIA VI, 10.

[22] *Itaque cum ille mentis aspectus, quem rationem vocamus, conjectus in rem aliquam, videt illam, scientia nominatur: cum autem non videt mens, quamvis intendat aspectum; inscitia vel ignorantia dicitur. De Quantitate Animae* (hereafter DQA) 27, 53.

[23] *...quod homo ad imaginem Dei factus dicitur, secundum interiorem hominem dici, ubi est ratio et intellectus... De Genesi Contra Manichaeos* I, 17, 28.

[24] *...Deus autem in ipsis rationalis animae secretis, qui homo interior vocatur... De Magistro* (hereafter DMA) I, 2.

[25] *...etiamsi quisquam contendat, quamvis nullum edamus sonum, tamen quia ipsa verba cogitamus, nos intus apud animum loqui...* DMA I, 2.

[26] *...in interiore homine habitat veritas... De Vera Religione* (hereafter DVR) XXXIX, 72.

[27] *...cor mundabit, quo visurus est Deum... De Sermone Domini in Monte* II, 12, 42.

28
   *Plerumque enim Scriptura cum os dicit,
conceptaculum ipsum cordis significat... De Mendacio*
(hereafter DME) 16, 31.
   29
   *Multa quippe homines faciunt ore clauso, quieta
lingua, voce frenata; sed tamen nihil agunt corposis
opere, quod non pruis dixerint corde. Ac per hoc
quoniam multa sunt peccata in interioribus dictis, quae
non sunt in exterioribus factis; nulla sunt autem in
exterioribus factis, quae non praecedant in interioribus
dictis: erit ab utrisque puritas innocentiae, si circum
interiora labia ponatur ostium continentiae. De
Continentia* (hereafter DC) II, 3.
   30
   *Et ecce corpus et anima in me mihi praesto sunt;
unum exterius, et alterum interius. Confessiones*
(hereafter CO) X, 6, 9.
   31
   *Quod ergo est ad corporis sensum aliquod corpus in
loco; hoc est ad animi aciem similitudo corporis in
memoria... De Trinitate* (hereafter DT) XI, 4, 7.
   32
   DT XII, 1, 1.
   33
   CO X, 6, 8.
   34
   ...res adhuc ad exteriorem hominem pertinens. DT
XII, 1, 1.
   35
   *...anima rationalis est mortali atque terreno
utens corpore. De Moribus Ecclesiae Catholicae et de
Moribus Manichaeorum* I, 27, 52.
   36
   *...descende in te, adi secretarium tuum, mentem
tuam... In Johannis Evangelium* (hereafter IJE) XXIII,
10; cf. DT X, 8, 11; IJE XXX VIII, 10.
   37
   ...non in te quasi in corpore tuo... IJE XXIII,
10; cf. DT X, 7, 10; DT IX, 3, 3.
   38
   *Redi ad cor; vide ibi quid sentias forte de Deo,
quia ibi est imago Dei. In interiore homine habitat*

Christus, in interiore homine renovanis ad imaginem Dei, in imagine sua cognosce auctorem ejus. IJE XVIII, 10.

[39] Cf. *De Diversis Quaestionibus* LXXXVI, 74. *Quaestinum in Heptateuchum* C, 4. Also, see R.A. Markus, "Augustine, Man: Body and Soul," *The Cambridge History of Later Greek and Early Medieval Philosophy* (Cambridge: Cambridge University Press, 1967), Chapter 22, especially pp. 360-361, and R.A. Markus, "'*Imago*' and '*similitudo*' in Augustine," *Review des etudes augustiniennes*, 1964.

[40] *Non...valde longe pergo in exempla, quando de mente tua volo aliquam similitudinem dare ad Deum tuum; quia utique non in corpore, sed in ipsa mente factus est Homo ad imaginem Dei.* IJE XXIII, 10. Cf. DT XIV, 12, 16; 16, 22; 17, 23.

[41] *Neque enim frustra et iste homo dicitur, nisi quia inest ei nonulla interioris similitudo.* DT XI, 1, 1. Cf. DT XIV, 10, 13.

[42] DC II, 4.

[43] *...corpus tuum non quod cor tuum; dimitte et corpus tuum, redi ad cor tuum.* IJE XVIII, 10.

[44] *...tanquam diceret: cum audis de ore, de corde intellige Utrumque dico; sed alterum ex altero expono, Habet os interius homo interior, et hoc discernit auris interior...* DC II, 4.

[45] *...qui corde laudat, interioris hominis voce laudat.* *Sermones* (hereafter SE) 257, 1.

[46] *...ipsa mens nostra, hoc est homo interior, ... quando immutabilem veritatem intelligit, eligit, dilligit, et lumen videt de quo dicitur, erat lumen verum; et verbum audit de quo dicitur, In principio erat verbum; et odorem capit de quo dicitur, Post*

odorem unguentorum tuorum curremus; et fontem bibit de
quo dicitur, Apud te est fons vitae; et tactu fruitur,
de quo dicitur, Mihi autem adhaerere Deo bonum est:...
IJE XCIX, 4.

47
De quibus ergo Dominus dicebat Qui habet aures
audiendi audiat?...An in corde no habes oculos? Unde
dicit Apostulus, Illuminatos oculos cordis vestri. IJE
XVIII, 10.

48
Una sententia duo quaedam hominis ora complexus
est, unum corporis, alterum cordis. DT XV, 10, 18.

49
Habetos interius homo interior, et hoc discernit
auris interior... DT II, 4.

50
In corpore tuo inveniebas alibi oculos, alibi
aures: in corde tuo numquid hoc invenis? IJE XVIII,
10.

51
...in ea substantia quae Deus est, non quasi per
corporis molem sensus locis propriis distributos...
IJE XCIX, 3.

52
Ostende mihi oculos, aures, nares cordes tui.
Diversa sunt quae ad cor tuum referuntur, et diversa ibi
membra non inveniuntur. IJE XVIII, 10.

53
In carne tua alibi audis, alibi vides: in corde
tuo ibi audis, ubi vides. IJE XVIII, 10.

54
Et videre et audire simul in Verbo est, nec aliud
est ibi audire, et aliud videre; sed auditus visus, et
visus auditus. IJE XVIII, 9.

55
...ibi sunt omnia; et videre, et audire, et
olfacere, et gustare, et tengere... IJE XCIX, 3.

56
Foris enim cum per corpus haec fiunt, aliud est
locutio, aliud visio: intus autem cum cogitamus,
utrumque unum est. Sicut auditio et visio duo quaedam

*sunt inter se distantia in sensibus corporis, in animo
autem non est aliud atque aliud videre aut audire: ac
per hoc cum locutio foris non videatur, sed potius
audiatur, locutiones tamen interiores, hoc est,
cogitationes visas dixit a Domino sanctum Evangelium,
non auditas...* DT XV, 10, 18.

[57] *...nec aliud atque aliud, sed una intelligentia
tot sensum nominibus, nuncupatur.* IJE XCIX, 4.

[58] Much of this discussion is based on Peter
Achinstein's *Concepts of Science* (Baltimore: The Johns
Hopkins Press, 1968) and *Law and Explanation* (London:
Oxford University Press, 1971); Max Black's *Models and
Metaphors* (Ithaca: Cornell University Press, 1962);
Marshall Spector's "Models and Theories," *British
Journal for the Philosophy of Science*, 1965.

Chapter 3
The Possibility of Knowledge
Si fallor, sum

I

One unique characteristic of philosophical
speculation is its involvement with apparently absurd
questions. As many philosophers have noted, this appearance of absurdity is due to ignorance of the problems that generate these questions. Further, it is
fairly obvious that many enduring philosophical questions are simply more sophisticated versions of questions people often ask in contemplative moments. "Is
knowledge possible?" is such a question. Any epistemologist worth his salt must confront this question and,
should he wish to construct a convincing epistemology,
answer it in the affirmative. Augustine is concerned
with traditional epistemological questions: What counts
as human knowledge? Is such knowledge possible? What
are the limits of such knowledge? My current concern
is with Augustine's argument for the possibility of
knowledge.

Augustine begins by knowing that knowledge is possible, and proceeds with an analysis of that knowledge.
However, this is not to suggest that Augustine never
confronts scepticism, for he clearly does. It is in
his confrontation with scepticism that we can see his
argument for the possibility of knowledge, as well as
his analysis of the extent to which one can doubt. His

general strategy in arguing for the possibility of
knowledge begins with a consideration of arguments that
are supposed to establish scepticism. Through a careful analysis of these arguments, Augustine then demonstrates that each sceptical line of reasoning in fact
requires at least the assumption of knowledge. This
strategy is familiar to readers of Descartes[1] who for
centuries have noticed striking similarities between
his *Cogito, ergo sum* and Augustine's *Si fallor, sum*.
The similarities are so striking, however, that few
have noticed that *Si fallor, sum*, as it occurs in its
various guises, provides a detailed analysis of error
and doubt that is philosophically consequential and
significant.

In this chapter I demonstrate that in the process
of establishing the possibility of knowledge, Augustine
uses *Si fallor, sum* to isolate a series of purely philosophical issues. How far may one rationally pursue
scepticism? (What is the reasonable scope of scepticism?) How are the various kinds of self-knowledge
interrelated? If one doubts the possibility of knowledge, what does such doubt entail? In the course of
considering these issues Augustine establishes *Si
fallor, sum* as a *series* of arguments having philosophical significance which transcends its importance as a
precursor of Descartes' *Cogito, ergo sum*.

II

Si fallor, sum refers to a series of arguments
Augustine provides at various stages in his philosophical development. The arguments occur at *De Civitate
Dei* X, 26; *De Trinitate* X, 10,14; *De Trinitate* XV, 12,
21 and *De Libero Arbitrio* 11, 3,7.[2] I will consider
each passage individually and then *Si fallor, sum* col-
lectively.

The most widely quoted occurrence of *Si fallor,
sum* is in *De Civitate Dei*.

...we are, and we know that we are, and
we love to be and to know that we are.
And in this...there is not a shadow of
illusion to disturb us...without any
illusion of image, fancy, or phantasm,
I am certain that I am, that I know that
I am, and that I love to be and to know.
   ...If (the sceptics) say 'What if you
are mistaken?' - well, if I am mistaken,
I am. For, if one does not exist, one
can by no means be mistaken. Therefore,
I am, if I am mistaken. Because, therefore, I am, if I am mistaken, how can I
be mistaken that I am, since it is certain
that I am, if I am mistaken. And because,
if I could be mistaken, I would have to be
the one who is mistaken, therefore, I am
most certainly not mistaken in knowing
that I am. Nor, as a consequence, am I
mistaken in knowing that I know. For,
just as I know that I am, I also know that
I know.[3]

This passage raises a number of issues crucial to
understanding *Si fallor, sum* and Augustine's epistemology. First, Augustine is maintaining that we have
privileged access to knowledge of self-existence. This
contrasts knowledge of self-existence with other kinds
of knowledge. For example, we gain knowledge of the
material world by means of an intermediary, a medium --
knowledge of the material world requires a mental image
representing that world. We call such knowledge mediate. The contrast, then, is between mediate knowledge
(for example, knowledge of the material world) and immediate knowledge (for example, knowledge of self-
existence). Error in such knowledge is a consequence

of the human inclination to reason from the media to
conclusions that the media do not entail. I have reliable knowledge of a particular image -- I know that it
seems to me as if there is a piece of paper before me --
but I can often go astray when I suppose that in fact
there *is* a piece of paper before me. Images may be il-
lusory or fanciful. Immediate knowledge does not encounter this difficulty, for immediate knowledge does
not require an intermediary. Knowledge of self-
existence is immediate. Since it is the medium that
can distort the message, the absence of a medium in
knowledge of self-existence vitiates the possibility of
error in such knowledge.

The second point to emphasize in considering this
passage from *De Civitate Dei* is that Augustine has not
conjured an argument for self-existence. Rather, the
argument is advanced for a specific purpose. Sceptics
have held that the possibility of being mistaken in
judgment undermines the possibility of ever knowing
with certainty. We shall see later that in the context
of knowledge of the physical world, Augustine recognizes
the error of requiring absolute certainty. *Si fallor,
sum* is aimed at sceptical arguments that allegedly
render knowledge impossible.

Third, the passage we are considering contains
several arguments. Each argument establishes a different point and advances Augustine's analysis of the
possibility of knowledge.

Argument I:

> (a) If one does not exist, then one cannot be
> mistaken.
>
> (b) If one could be mistaken, then one does
> exist.
>
> (c) If one is in fact mistaken, then one exists.

Thus, (d) If I am mistaken, then I exist.

    (e) Either I am correct, or I am mistaken.

    (f) I exist.

The reasoning in this argument is fairly straight-forward.

    (a) If one does not exist, then one cannot be mistaken. If one does not exist, then one cannot be anything at all except non-existent. It follows that one thing a non-existent person cannot be is mistaken.

    (b) If it is possible for one to be mistaken, then one does exist. This follows from (a) by contraposition. The possibility of being in error entails existence, for one who is non-existent cannot be in error (or anything else).

    (c) If one is in fact mistaken, then one exists. (c) is entailed by (b) by means of a straight-forward modal principle: Actuality entails possibility. The modal principle asserts if in fact ϕ, then it is possible ϕ. (b) asserts, If possible ϕ, then ψ. Thus, if in fact ϕ, then ψ.

    (d) If I am mistaken, then I exist. This follows from (c) *A fortiori*; if it is true that for any-one being mistaken entails existence, it is true for me as well.

    (e) This is tautological.

Argument I is the central argument for the existence of the self that is offered by Augustine. The other arguments in this passage from *De Civitate Dei* also appear to establish the existence of the self. In fact, they support the central argument and go beyond it.

Argument II:

    (a) If I am mistaken, then I am.

Thus, (b) I am certain that I am.

The inference of (b) from (a) is not so obvious as the inferences in Argument I. We may fill in the argument for Augustine by adding the following suppressed premises.

      (a) If I am correct, then I am.

      (a'') If I am correct or I am mistaken, then I am. (If p entails q and r entails q, then p or r entails q.)

      (a''') I am either correct or I am mistaken. (Is there a third possibility?)

Thus, (b) I am certain that I am (from a'' and a''' by *modus ponens*).

    With Argument II Augustine expands upon the conclusion to Argument I. The conclusion to Argument I is a simple assertion of self-existence. The context in which these Arguments are presented is one in which it is maintained that knowledge of self-existence is incorrigible because it is immediate. Argument I established self-existence. However, that argument did not provide the epistemic status of such knowledge -- it did not provide an account of the degree to which such knowledge is supported. Argument II makes a claim about the epistemic status of knowledge of self-existence; such knowledge is certain. The scope of *Fallor* is expanded, by Argument II, to include an assertion about the status of the knowledge of self-existence.

Argument III:

      (a) If I am correct, then I am the one who is correct.

      (b) If I am mistaken, then I am the one who is mistaken.

      (c) I am in some epistemic state whether I am mistaken or correct.

      (d) In order to be in an epistemic state I have to exist.

Thus, (e) I know that I am.

The reasoning here is obvious enough to require no furthur elaboration. What is not obvious is the justification for (e), Augustine's assertion that he knows
that he exists. This step in the argument has made
Professor Gareth Matthews uneasy.

> ...it {this argument} has a fatal flaw...
> whereas {this argument yields} the con-
> clusion "I am," Augustine's answer to the
> Academic skeptics is supposed to vouchsafe
> "I know that I am."
>
> Could one use the same form of argument
> to support "I know that I am?" No.[4]

Professor Matthews' criticism proceeds as follows:
Augustine has provided us with reasons for asserting
"I exist." However, he has not provided reasons for
asserting "I know that I exist." The conclusion of the
argument is an epistemic claim -- a claim to know.
Previous steps in the argument do not support the claim
to know in any obvious way.

This argument is problematic because it is advanced in an epistemic context. Augustine wishes to
draw an epistemic conclusion from an argument con-
taining no epistemic premise. What must be seen is
that Augustine is here writing about the justification
I have for my own knowledge claims; under what circumstances am I justified in claiming "I know p." Clearly,
these will be circumstances in which I believe that a
particular knowledge claim has a strong justification,
whether that justification in fact justifies p. In
this context, the Gettier paradoxes do not arise.

There is another, more crucial problem which is
central to the criticism and arises in an analysis of
knowledge claims that has generated much attention in
recent literature.

The standard analysis of the sentence 'x knows p'
involves three elements. x has to believe p. x has to
have good and adequate reasons for the belief that p.
'p' has to be true. Augustine believes that he exists,
and he thinks that *Fallor* provides him with good and
adequate reasons for his belief. Professor Matthews,
however, seems to want Augustine to do something else
before he is allowed to say, "I know that I exist."
Presumably, Augustine must show that it is true that he
exists (for this is the only element in the standard
analysis that is lacking). I shall argue that to require that Augustine (or anyone else) provide a justification for a belief and to require that the belief
also be true is dialectically redundant; no one would
or should expect both from a putative knower.

Suppose that I am concerned to determine whether a
person x knows p. On the standard view I would begin
by determining whether x believes p. Next, following
the traditional analysis, I would attempt to determine
whether x has good and adequate reasons for his belief
that p. Reasons are good and adequate when they are
the best or the most complete reasons currently available. (x does not know that the earth is spherical if
his belief is based upon his other belief that the
earth is a gigantic orange. If there are no good and
adequate reasons that *can* be given for the belief, then
x does not know p, and neither does anyone else.)

Having established that x believes p and that he
has good and adequate reasons for his belief, the standard analysis next requires that 'p' be true. What are
we to make of this requirement? If someone asked x
whether 'p' is true, x would assert that 'p' is true.
If x were required to support his assertion, he would
provide those good and adequate reasons he has for his
belief that p. There is nothing else that p could do,

nor can any reasonable person expect x to do anything else in support of his claim that 'p' is true. 'p is true' is simply a telescoped version of all of the best justifications that can be given for 'p', and to support the claim that 'p' is true is to extend the telescope; it is to give those justifications. It is, of course, possible to know that something is true without being able to provide the (telescoped) justifications. The point here is not one about knowing (one cannot know without a justification) but about something's being true. Thus, I can say, "I know that Pluto is beyond the orbit of Neptune," without ever having seen either Pluto or Neptune, because I take as authoritative a book on astronomy. To take it as authoritative is to suppose that the author is able to provide a justification. Thus, in *supporting* the claim a justification must be possible. Thus, it is dialectically absurd to include in the proper analysis of 'x knows p' both the requirement that the claim is justified and the requirement that it is true, for the inclusion of the truth requirement is redundant. Once x has provided the best available support for p -- once he is warranted in asserting "p" -- he adds nothing by asserting, 'and "p" is also true.'

If my argument is correct, then Augustine is justified in maintaining that he knows that he exists on the basis of his having established his existence. Thus, he can get "I know that I exist" as the conclusion of the same argument that leads to "I exist."

Fallor in *De Civitate Dei* accomplishes several tasks. First, it serves as a response to sceptical claims about the impossibility of knowledge by demonstrating that something -- the fact of self-existence -- can be known. Second, it demonstrates that such knowledge is presented in a special way; it is

immediate. Third, it shows that such knowledge is very
strongly grounded -- it is certain. Finally, it shows
that this bit of knowledge is, in fact, known.

The next passage to consider is *De Trinitate* X, 10,
14. "...who would doubt that he lives, remembers,
understands, wills, thinks, knows and judges? For, even
if he doubts, he lives..."[5] It is in this passage that
Augustine develops the surprising implications of
Fallor. He begins with a repetition of the essential
element in Argument I. The first sentence in the passage quoted, however, is then developed in detail.
This development takes *Fallor* beyond the scope of the
three arguments presented above.

> ...if he doubts, he remembers why he
> doubts; if he doubts, he understands
> that he doubts; if he doubts, he wishes
> to be certain; if he doubts, he thinks;
> if he doubts, he knows that he does not
> know; if he doubts, he judges that he
> ought not to consent rashly. Whoever
> then doubts about anything else ought
> never to doubt about all of these; for
> if they were not, he would be unable to
> doubt anything at all.[6]

In the passages considered above, Augustine offered
Fallor as a reply to scepticism; his concern was to
establish the possibility of knowledge. Basic to *Fallor*
is doubt -- a psychological phenomenon -- and in the
present passage Augustine turns his attention to the
relationship between the psychological and the epistemological. His examination takes the form of a series of
inferences that are based upon the simple act of doubting. He maintains that if he doubts, then there are a
number of things that he knows with certainty (he
"...ought never to doubt about all of these..."). What

follows is a review of each stage of Augustine's analysis.

As I shall argue in Chapter 4, Augustine takes memory to be central to all other knowledge. Characteristically, he begins his analysis of doubt by considering the role played by memory in doubting. If he doubts, then he must remember why he doubts. Underlying this inference is a theme that connects all elements of his analysis of doubt: one does not doubt in a vacuum -- the concern is with what I shall call rational doubt. I take rational doubt to be doubt that results from thoughtful reflection, as contrasted with simple petulant gainsaying. For example, a sceptical argument would provide the basis for rational doubt. Rational doubt, then, involves reason or reflection. The rational doubter continues to doubt because he bears the product of reason or reflection in mind.

If he doubts, then he understands that he doubts. Once again Augustine is establishing a particular epistemic state as being associated with *Fallor*. Doubt is a state that one is aware of; it is conscious ("He doubts *P*, but doesn't know that he doubts *P*", would seem an absurdity.) Thus, the doubter knows that he doubts. (One might say that for doubting, *esse* is *percipi*.)[7]

If he doubts, he wishes to be certain. Again, Augustine is writing of rational doubt. Suppose that doubt is due to a sceptical argument. Sceptical consequences will only follow from an argument if there is an antecedent desire -- a desire to know. One who did not desire knowledge of a particular sort would not be taken by scepticism. For example, an argument demonstrating the impossibility of knowing whether the inhabitants of the Andaman Islands will use Saran Wrap as a medium of exchange in 1,000 years would not disturb me,

as I do not care about the economy of the Andamans in
1,000 years. The problems raised by doubt are problems
for one who wishes to know. One who does not wish to
know will be unconcerned by the possibility of error.

If one doubts, one thinks. Again, Augustine is
concerned with what I have been calling rational doubt.
The act of doubting requires the doubter to think.
However, the inference is not simply "to doubt is to
think." The earlier elements of the analysis -- memory,
understanding, wishing to be certain -- and the later
elements -- knowing one does not know, and judging --
are thinking. Thus, if doubting entails these other
things, and each of these is an example of thinking,
then doubting entails thinking.

If one doubts, then he knows that he does not know.
This inference emphasizes one of the central requirements for doubt. A precondition for scepticism is the
recognition that we sometimes mistakenly think that we
know. We know, then, that there are times when we do
not know. If one were unaware of the possibility of
ignorance or error -- of not-knowing -- then one would
not doubt.

If one doubts, then one judges that one ought not
to consent rashly. This strikes me as Augustine's most
interesting observation about doubt. The important and
legitimate message of scepticism is that we ought to be
cautious about our knowledge. Often, scepticism -- the
possibility that I might be mistaken in a particular
judgment -- is taken to justify never consenting to a
belief. Scepticism is supposed to make knowledge impossible in every case. But it is one thing to take
doubt and the possibility of error seriously, it is
quite another to think that they undermine knowledge of
any sort. Augustine here asserts that we ought to
judge with care and reflection, bearing in mind the

possibility of error. It seems to me that as a
consequence Augustine may be saying that we can judge
even in the presence of doubt.

   De Trinitate X, 10,14 contains Augustine's analysis
of doubt. If one is to take doubt seriously, then one
is to take these inferences seriously. In a passage
that is not a statement of *Fallor*, although it is similar in form, Augustine asserts another epistemic consequence of doubting. In *De Vera Religione* Augustine
maintains that, "Everyone who knows that he doubts also
knows with certainty something true, namely, that he
doubts."[8] There is a similar passage at *Contra
Academicos* III, 9,18-19, in which Augustine argues that
the academicians are wrong in saying that nothing can
be known, since the basis for that assertion (i.e.,
Zeno's notion that what can be apprehended has nothing
in common with what is false) is either true, in which
case something is known to be true, or it is false, in
which case it ought not to lead anyone to doubt anything.

   In *De Trinitate* XV, 12,21 Augustine presents his
most completely epistemological treatment of *Fallor*.

>   First of all, the knowledge itself
>   from which our thought is truly formed,
>   and when we say what we know, of what
>   sort is it, and how much can a man, even
>   of the most extraordinary skill and
>   learning acquire?...
>   It is an inner knowledge by which we
>   know that we live, where not even the
>   academician can say: 'Perhaps you are
>   sleeping, and you do not know, and you
>   see in dreams'. For who does not know
>   that things seen by those who are asleep
>   are very similar to things seen by those

who are awake. But he who is certain
about the knowledge of his own life does
not say in it: 'I know that I am awake',
but 'I know that I live'; whether he,
therefore, sleeps, or whether he is awake,
he lives. He cannot be deceived in his
knowledge of this even by dreams, because
to sleep and see in dreams is characteristic of one who lives. Nor can the
academician argue as follows against this
knowledge: 'Perhaps you are insane, and
do not know it, because the things seen by
the sane are very similar to those seen by
the insane, but he who is insane lives';
nor does he make this retort to the academicians: 'I know that I am not insane',
but 'I know that I live'. He can never,
therefore, be deceived nor lie who says
that he knows that he lives. Let a thousand
kind of optical illusions be placed before
one who says: 'I know that I live'; he will
fear none of them, since even he who is
deceived, lives.[9]

There is much going on in this passage. Augustine
begins with two central epistemological questions.
What is human knowledge? What are the limits of that
knowledge? Sceptics lead us to believe that we ought
to doubt everything. Augustine presents the traditional problem of appearance and reality (...wherein so
many things are different from what they seem...) by
means of a familiar argument -- the dream argument.
His remarks on dreaming are presented as an argument
because he is concerned with rational doubt.

    (a) People see things while awake.
    (b) People see in dreams.

(c) Things seen by those who are asleep are very similar to things seen by those who are awake.

(d) Perhaps you are sleeping and you do not know. Thus, (e) You must doubt the testimony of the senses. In reply to this sceptical argument Augustine changes the focus of concern. He suggests that in this context the testimony of the senses be ignored as a source of knowledge. But, he goes on, this does not entail that as a result of the dream argument we are epistemically destitute, for there are things that we know. In fact, those other things that we know serve as a standard for our putative knowledge claims.[10] What we know is *not* "I am awake" nor is it "I am not insane" but "I am alive." No matter what phenomena are used by the sceptic, none can undermine the certainty of "I am alive" since the existence of the person who is allegedly deceived is assumed by all of the sceptic's tricks. Knowledge of self-existence, then, is unlike knowledge of the physical world. Self-existence is known in a special way -- it is inner-knowledge. Since it is purely inner, it is certain.

This assertion of the inner nature of knowledge of self-existence echoes *De Civitate Dei* XI, 26, where Augustine maintains that knowledge of the existence of the self is immediate or direct. The privileged nature of self-knowledge in general is developed at *De Trinitate* X. "...when it is said to the mind: 'Know thyself', it knows itself at the very instant in which it understands the word 'thyself', and it knows itself for no other reason than that it is present to itself."[11]

One of Augustine's central goals in *De Trinitate* is to establish the possibility of knowledge. The genesis of all knowledge is inner, whether it is attained through the offices of illumination or by the effects of the putative knower. Most of Augustine's

writing on *Fallor* is inferential. However, when he
discusses self-knowledge he appeals to the inner nature
of knowledge. Inner knowledge is gained by the knower
solely through his own efforts. Thus, the knowledge [12]
that one exists is performative.

III

There are several arguments and motives central to
Fallor. Augustine's principal reason for advancing the
argument is to establish the possibility of knowledge
in light of sceptical arguments to the contrary. He
maintains that knowledge of one's existence is attained
in a special way which is unlike the way we learn about
the material world. Because this knowledge is attained
in a special way it is not liable to error. Thus,
knowledge of one's own existence is certain. This sort
of knowledge also has a special status in Augustine's
broader epistemology, for it serves as a standard in [13]
terms of which other knowledge might be judged.

Augustine's *Fallor*, as an inference, establishes
the same conclusion as the *Cogito*. *Fallor* also has a
performance aspect, insofar as awareness of the existence of the self is inner-knowledge for Augustine.
Fallor is significant for two reasons. First,
Augustine maintains that *Fallor* supports a specific
series of knowledge claims. Second, Augustine is concerned with an analysis of doubt. Rather than using
the possibility of doubt simply as a starting point for
the development of a positive epistemology, Augustine
confronts the reality of doubt and considers what sorts
of things can be known simply on the basis of that
reality. This analysis is philosophically significant
and important for its own sake.

Knowledge is possible, then, because even those
attempts to demonstrate that it is impossible require
knowing something. Now we turn our attention to

Augustine's positive epistemology, beginning with a discussion of his treatment of memory.

Chapter 3

Footnotes

[1] Some philosophers have argued that Augustine and
Descartes are involved in essentially dissimilar enter-
prises.

> Augustine's *si fallor, sum* is thus not an
> argument, or part of an argument, intended
> to establish that one exists. Since
> Descartes' *cogito, ergo sum* is such an ar-
> gument..., Augustine's reasoning is basically,
> and not just incidentially, different from
> Descartes'.
> (Gareth B. Matthews, "*Si fallor, Sum,*" in
> *Augustine: A Collection of Critical Essays*,
> edited by R.A. Markus, Doubleday, Anchor,
> 1972, p. 161.)

Professor Matthews tells us that Descartes does something with the *Cogito* that Augustine does not do with
the *Fallor*. Because they are used differently they are
not the same argument.

> ...Descartes is distinguished from most of
> his predecessors by his awareness of the
> performatory character of his first and
> foremost insight...In so far as I know,
> there is no indication that Augustine was
> ever alive to the possibility of inter-
> preting his version of the *Cogito* as a
> performance rather than as an inference or
> as a factual observation...What he dwells
> on is merely the "impossibility of thinking
> without existing."
> (Jaakko Hintikka, "*Cogito, Ergo Sum*:
> Inference or Performance?" in *Descartes: A
> Collection of Critical Essays*, edited by

Willis Doney, Doubleday Anchor, 1967,
pp. 129-130.)
Professor Hintikka maintains that Descartes took the
Cogito to be a performance; to be something that one
does for one's self. This is to contrast it with an inference; with something that is generalizable.
Augustine was unaware of the possibility of using
Fallor in the way Descartes uses it. Presumably, *Fallor*
is an inference.

Not to put too fine a point on things, Descartes himself noticed similarities.

> I am obliged to you for drawing my attention
> to the passage of St. Augustine relevant to
> my *I am thinking, therefore I exist*...I find
> that he really does use it to prove the cer-
> tainty of our existence. He goes on to show
> that there is a certain likeness of the
> Trinity in us, in that we exist, and we love
> the existence and the knowledge we have. I,
> on the other hand, use the argument to show
> that this I which is thinking is an immaterial
> substance with no bodily element. These are
> two very different things. In itself it is
> such a simple and natural thing to infer that
> one exists from the fact that one is doubting
> that it could have occurred to any writer.
> (*Descartes: Philosophical Letters*, trans-
> lated and edited by Anthony Kenny, Clarendon
> Press Oxford, 1970, p. 84.)

[2] The argument at SO II, 1, 1 is a peculiar one. A
number of scholars think that this argument is a precursor of Descartes' *Cogito, ergo sum*. Augustine
simply argues that from an admission of ignorance one
can know what one thinks. Although later in the second
book of SO he states that one knows that one lives, he
doesn't argue for it.

[3]
Nam et sumus et nos esse novimus et esse ac nosse diligimus. In his autem tribus quae dixi, nulla nos falsitas veri similis turbat...sed sine ulla phantasmatum imagionatione ludificatoria mihi esse me idque nosse et amare certissimum est.

Nulla in his veris Academicorum argumenta formido dicentium, Quid si falleris? Si enim fallor, sum. Nam qui non est, utique nec falli potest; ac per hoc sum, si fallor. Quia ergo sum si fallor, quo modo esse me fallor, quando certum est me esse, si fallor? Quia igitur essem qui fallerer, etiamsi fallerer, procul dubio in eo quod me novi esse, non fallor. Consequens est autem ut etiam in eo quod me novi nosse, non fallar. Sicut enim novi esse me, ita novi etiam hoc ipsum, nosse me. De Civitate Dei (hereafter DCD) XI, 26 (Fathers of the Church Translation).

[4]
Matthews, "*Si fallor, sum*," p. 157.

[5]
Vivere se tamen et meminisse, et intelligere, et velle, et cogitare, et scire, et judicare quis dubitet? Quandoquidem etiam si dubitat, vivit... DT X, 10, 14 (Fathers of the Church Translation).

[6]
...si dubitat unde dubitet, meminit; si dubitat, dubitare se intelligit; si dubitat, certus esse vult; si dubitat, cogitat; si dubitat, scit se nescire; si dubitat, judicat non se temere consentire aportere. Quisquis igitur aliunde dubitat, de his omnibus dubitare non debet: quae si non essent, de ulla re dubitare non posset. DT X, 10, 14.

[7]
A necessary and sufficient condition for doubting is simply to doubt.

[8]
Omnis qui se dubitemtem intelligit, verum intelligit, et de hac re quam intelligit certus est: de vero igitur certus est. Omnis igitur qui utrum sit

veritas dubitat, in seipso habet verum unde non dubitet; nec ullum verum nisi veritate verum est. DVR 39, 73 (Author's Translation).

[9] *Primo ipsa scientia, de qua veraciter cogitatio nostra formatur, quando quae scimus loquimur, qualis aut quanta potest homini provenire, quamlibet peritissimo atque doctissimo?*

Intima scientia est qua non vivere scimus, ubi he illud quidem Academicus dicere potest: Fortasse dormis, et nescis, et in somnis vides. Visa quippe sumniantium simillima esse visis vigilantium quis ignorat? Sed qui certus est de vitae suae scientia, non in ea dicit, Scio me vigilare; sed, Scio me vivere: sire ergo dormiat, sive vigilet, vivit. Nec in ea scientia per somnia falli potest; quia et dormire et in somnis videre, viventis est. Nec illud potest Academicus adversus istam scientiam dicere. Furis fortassis et nescis; quia sanorum visis simillima sunt etiam visa furentium: sed qui furit vivit. Nec contra Academicos dicit, Scio me non furere; sed, Scio me vivere. Nunquam ergo falli nec mentiri potest, qui se vivere dixerit scire. Mille itaque fallacium visorum genera objiciantur ei qui dicit, Scio me vivere; nihil horum timebit, quando et qui fallitur vivit. DT XV, 12, 21.

[10] Augustine treats the ideas gained by illumination as standards for judgment at many places including *De Genesi ad Litteram* (hereafter DGAL) XII, 24.

[11] *Sed cum dicitur menti, Cognosce te ipsam, eo ictu quo intelligit quod dictum est, te ipsam, cognoscit se ipsam; nec ob aliud, quam eo quod sibi praesens est.* DT X, 9, 12.

[12] There is one further version of *Fallor* worth mentioning. It is offered in *De Libero Arbitro* II, 3, 7. Augustine reassures Evodius with a question.

"Possibly, you are afraid of being mistaken by this
kind of question when, actually, you could not be mistaken at all if you did not exist?" This is another
version of Argument I, with the additional conclusion
that one could not be wrong in thinking that one exists.
*An tu fortasse metuis, he in hac interrogatione fallaris,
cum utique si non esses, falli omnino non posses?*
[13]
Augustine would include this knowledge among those
things that are known through illumination. The principal ideas that illumination provide serve as a standard or template for knowledge, since they are
representations of Divine Ideas.

Chapter 4
Memory

The majority of our knowledge claims are not about
the present. Most claims are either about the past (as
when we talk about the course of the Battle of Gettys-
burg) or they require correlation of claims about the
past (as when we discuss the present state of Germany)
or they require that we bear in mind a number of different notions (as when we speculate about the future
of manned space-flight). The majority of our knowledge
claims rely upon memory in one way or another. We expect an epistemologist, then, to have quite a bit to
say about memory.

St. Augustine discusses memory in its many guises.
The problem is that his analysis of memory is often
presented in a manner that makes it *prima facie* im-
plausible. I do three things in this chapter. First,
I outline Augustine's account of memory. Second, I
present some general remarks about memory. In particular, I describe the classical problems that any theory
of memory has to face. Third, I show that Augustine's
comments on memory are reasonable and that his analysis
of memory renders moot some of the classical sceptical
arguments aimed at the justification of memory.

Memoria is central to and crucial in Augustine's
epistemology. He uses the word in two different contexts. Sometimes he uses *memoria* as we would use
"memory." Other times he uses the word as we would use

"conception," or "imagination." There are three elements in Augustine's analysis of memory that support the
second, broader use of *memoria*. First, his suggestion
that our knowledge of the past is much like our knowledge of the present. Second, his view that *memoria* is
central to the analysis of all knowledge claims. Third,
his insistence that mental images are the media for
memories, which has been taken to mean that for
Augustine memory reports are *about* mental images. I
shall argue that problems raised by the first two peculiarities in his analysis are only apparent and that
the criticism annexed to the third is unsympathetic. I
shall begin by setting out the issues that I take to be
important for an understanding of Augustine on memory.
Augustine's analysis is contrary to the frequently encountered suggestion that memory is essentially different from other kinds of knowledge and that, because of
this difference, memory claims require a special justification. Recent epistemologists hint that memory is
not different from other sorts of knowledge and that
all knowledge *requires* memory. I shall digress from my
discussion of Augustine to make explicit the details
and implications of these hints. Finally, I shall argue for the merits of Augustine's view. I hope to show
that Augustine's use of *memoria* reveals an analysis of
memory that rewards close scrutiny.

I

Recent memory theorists have pointed out that
there are several different sorts of memory. Since
some philosophers have been criticized for confusing
the different ways in which "memory" may be used it is
important to indicate what Augustine was accounting for
in his analysis of memory.

Augustine holds that factual memory (memory that)
and personal memory (memory of) are closely tied. He

writes to Nebridius that, "When I remember my father, I likewise remember that he left me and is no longer alive; when I remember Carthage, I recall that it still exists and that I left it."[1] I shall be primarily concerned with Augustine's treatment of factual memory for two reasons. First, it is in his discussion of factual memory that Augustine presents views about memory that are closest to contemporary discussions. Second, I agree with contemporary writers that a correct analysis of factual memory is at the core of an analysis of other kinds of memory.

Augustine's analysis of factual and personal memory is unabashedly representational. When he remembers his dead father and Carthage, "...neither of these things can come into memory without that mental picture."[2] To remember is to attend to an image which is immediate to the inner eye and which represents some previous experience. This object is "stored" in the memory and is "called up" by the mind when remembered.

> Further, there is stored in the memory
> the thoughts we think by adding to or
> taking from, or otherwise modifying, the
> things that sense has made contact with,
> and all other things that have been en-
> trusted to and laid up in memory, save
> such as forgetfulness has swallowed in
> its grave. When I turn to memory, I ask
> it to bring forth what I want. And some
> things are produced immediately. Some
> take longer as if they had been brought
> out of some secret place of storage.
> Some pour out in a heap. And while we
> are actually wanting and looking for
> something quite different, they hurl
> themselves upon us in masses, as if to

> say, "May it not be we that you want?"
> I brush them from the face of my memory
> with the hand of my heart, until at
> last the thing that I want is brought to[3]
> light as from some hidden place.

When I remember, memory offers up candidates which I
may in turn consider. I review each candidate and
either accept or reject it. The mechanism of review,
acceptance, or rejection, is inner vision, which takes
as its object "...the likeness of the body which the
memory retains...."[4]

This discussion concerns the nature of memory phenomena. In recent literature on memory the phenomenological problem (What goes on in the mind when one
remembers?) has been criticized as non-philosophical.
Although I am concerned here with the epistemological
status and role of memory, there is an interesting relationship between imagery and Augustine's account of
memory which I shall discuss below.

One way to get at the central issues in Augustine's
analysis of memory is to consider a recent criticism of
his account of memory claims. This is a profitable
strategy because Augustine's linguistic theory closely
ties factual memory to memory reports. Professor
Gareth Matthews argues that "Augustine seems to be
saying that whenever we are asked about familiar but
absent sensible things we respond by changing the subject..."[5] As evidence for this analysis of Augustine's
view of memory claims, Professor Matthews quotes:

> When a question arises not about what
> we sense before us but about what we
> have sensed in the past, then we do
> not speak of things themselves but of
> images impressed from them on the mind[6]
> and committed to memory.

As Professor Matthews points out, the language of
this passage is quite peculiar. Augustine seems to imply that when one speaks of *present* material objects
one is speaking of things themselves, while talk about
familiar but absent material objects is talk about
images (or, such talk requires as intermediary some sort
of mental image). Further, there are two ways one can
take the question, "How can we answer questions about
sensible things from memory?" One way is to suppose
that it is a request for an explanation of the mental
mechanism which makes it possible for us to speak of
things from memory (the phenomenological problem). The
other way is to take it to be a question about how a
response counts as answering a question about absent
sensible things. For Professor Matthews, talking about
mental images is one way of explaining how we are able
to answer questions about absent sensible things. However, when it comes to showing *why* a memory claim is a
good answer to a question about sensible things,
Augustine's analysis will not work because a memory
claim must be liable to confirmation or disconfirmation.
When we confirm or disconfirm we appeal to the memories
of others or to some other standard. Whatever we do,
we do not talk about our own mental images, but, rather,
about things themselves.

There are a number of points worth attending to in
response to Professor Matthews' paper. First, Professor Matthews is correct in maintaining that

> It will not be satisfactory to say that
> a response based upon a look at one's
> memory images automatically counts as
> answering a question about absent sensi-
> ble things. What the respondent says
> must be made liable to confirmation and
> disconfirmation by evidence other than

> the "proof" of his own memory images
> if it is to count as an answer to a
> question about absent sensible things
> (and not merely as a report of the
> respondent's sense impressions).[7]

However, this criticism may be applied to *any* memory
claim, whether or not a representative theory is assumed. In questioned or questionable cases it is simply not enough to establish that something happened in
the past by relying on one's memory, whether it is
"grounded" in images or in something else. Further,
this criticism may be applied to any knowledge claim
whether it is a claim about an absent or a present object. If I say, "I parked at the corner of 63rd and
Main," or "This piece of paper is white," my statements
stand, with no furthur elaboration, *unless* someone
calls them into question. If someone questions a claim
that I make about a *present* object it won't do for me
to support my claim by reporting whatever my impressions are at the moment. More is necessary. Indeed, I
will appeal to the object itself, as Professor Matthews
suggests.

As to the claim that when we speak about absent
but familiar objects we respond by changing the subject,
Professor Matthews is correct. In fact, Augustine's
analysis of talk about absent objects involves images.
In the same sense, however, talk about *present* material
objects is talk "about" images. Further, for Augustine
an image in memory plays a role in *all* knowledge
claims, so changing the subject is a characteristic of
all knowledge claims, not just memory claims.

II

I have already suggested that all knowledge claims
involve memory. For the sake of contrast, however, I
wish to distinguish between knowledge of the past and

knowledge of the present, between remembered knowledge and acquired knowledge. A distinction may also be drawn between immediate acquisition (or memory), situations in which knowledge results from direct experience (whether of a dissected frog, a battle, a famous person, a toothache), and mediate acquisition (or memory) -- knowledge gained through a medium (a book, newspaper, lecture).

Epistemologists often treat memory knowledge as though it were prone to difficulties not shared by acquisition knowledge. These difficulties are most often advanced in terms of a scepticism regarding the reliability of memory as evidence for events occurring in the past, a scepticism to which acquisition knowledge is allegedly immune. This scepticism, when aimed at a representative account of memory such as Augustine's, is generally taken to have three sources.

If we characterize whatever it is that one attends to immediately when remembering as a "memory presentation," then the first reason that memory is allegedly unreliable is because memory presentations are sometimes inadequate. This inadequacy may be represented formally as follows.

When a person P makes a memory claim at T_2 about some previous state S which occurred at T_1, the claim at T_2 has as evidence E something true of that person at T_2. In terms of a representative account we may call what it is that is true of the person at T_2 a "memory presentation." It is the inadequacy of memory presentations that is the first source of scepticism about memory. The presentation may be inadequate in that it omits key aspects of S while including enough about S to indicate to P that he is not remembering everything about S. The memory presentation may be inadequate in another way, for it may be initially

inadequate but may lead P, through self-correction, to
provide a more complete account of S. The first sort of
inadequacy undermines confidence in memory as giving
complete knowledge, the second sort of inadequacy may
lead P to wonder whether the claim made at T_2 will in
turn be undermined by some further correcting memory at
T_3.

The second reason memory is taken to be unreliable
is because it is possible that E is not evidence for S
but is, in fact, some other mental phenomenon. Mnemon-
ic hallucination has been recognized as a problem for
memory theory since Aristotle. The problem is given
plausibility by the recognition that P cannot know
whether E is imagined or whether E is evidence for S.
In fact, this problem is apparently two-edged, for it
is possible that P might dismiss E as imagined when it
is good evidence for S.

The third reason memory is taken to be unreliable
is that we make temporal errors, either remembering an
event as having occurred at one time, when in fact it
occurred at another time, or misremembering the sequence
of a series of events.

As has often happened in the history of epistemology, these sceptical considerations have been so influ-
ential that memory theory has become almost exclusively
a running battle with scepticism. Because it is
thought that there are certain peculiar epistemological
problems that are unique to memory, philosophers who
wish to defend the reliability of memory knowledge have
spent a good deal of time and effort searching for
special memory marks ("memory flags" or "memory indicators") which would guarantee that what is true of P
at T_2 will be evidence for S. These "flags" or "indicators" are taken to be some peculiar properties of
memory presentations (some peculiar mental phenomena)

which distinguish such presentations from other
phenomena (for example, imagination).

The mistake here is to suppose that the difficulties sketched above are unique to memory. In fact,
these are tokens of difficulties that have raised problems for acquired knowledge as well. As Augustine recognized, memory is central to knowledge. Thus, the
search for memory indicators is justified, although, as
I shall argue, that search is carried out in the wrong
place. There are memory indicators, but these indicators are not aspects or qualities of (for example)
memory presentations.

The testimony of the senses plays a role for immediately acquired knowledge that is similar to the role
played by the memory presentation (or its equivalent
for non-representational theories) in memory knowledge.
Inadequacy of the memory presentation was taken to be
the first source of scepticism for memory. For immediate acquisition it is certainly possible (common) to
see just enough or to hear just enough of a contemporary
state to know that what is seen or heard is not all that
there is to be seen or heard. Perceptual knowledge is
self-correcting in the same way that memory knowledge
is. We are always prepared to modify our beliefs about
the world through examination of the world, and here,
too, one can never be certain that a future experience
will not undermine a particular belief we currently
hold. As to mediately acquired knowledge, we may be
told just enough, or we may read just enough, to know
that we do not have the full story, and everyone has
had the experience of modifying a previous claim by
being told more.

We may view the second allegedly unique source of
problems for memory similarly. Thus, because it is
possible to confuse memory presentations with other

mental phenomena (most notoriously, imagination) we are
supposed to hold that memory is unreliable. After all,
the reason that I think that I walked here this morning
may be because I imagine that I walked. But there are
counterparts to this source of scepticism in acquisition situations. Since I can hallucinate, imagine,
hear voices and so on it is obviously possible for me
to mistake an illusion for a genuine experience. If
the genuine experience is strange enough, I can even
mistake a genuine experience for an illusion. If these
sorts of mistakes can be made when acquiring knowledge,
then it appears that this second source of scepticism
is not unique to memory knowledge.

The third class of memory problems, those arising
from temporal errors regarding the sequence of events,
seems to have the *prima facie* strongest claim to being
unique to memory. For one thing, it is hard to decide
whether to classify temporal errors as inadequacy of
memory content, or as a mistake of memory presentation.
Do I think that the television set was purchased before
the record player because the content of the memory
presentation is inadequate, or because I am mistaking
an imagined memory for a real memory? What makes temporal errors even more unusual is the absence of any
obvious parallel in contemporary learning cases. I may
make mistakes about what the time is right now, but I
will not suppose that, whatever time it is, my current
experience is being had at some other time.

Of all of the types of error, temporal errors seem
to be the only ones that are unique to memory, having
no parallel in errors that might be made in contemporary learning situations. That temporal errors are
unique to memory should not be too surprising, since it
is precisely memory that is supposed to provide us with
a faculty to relate events temporally.

So far, upon examination, the reasons that memory
is supposed to be prone to a peculiar epistemological
unease turn out (with one exception) to be reasons for
unease about acquisition as well. However, there re-
main two special problems for memory. One problem is
tied to an alleged difficulty in distinguishing between
memories and imaginations. The second problem is tied
to ways in which memory claims can (or cannot) be veri-
fied or supported and it depends upon the indispens-
ability of memory in supporting a memory claim. I
shall consider both difficulties together.

A memory claim may be tested in two ways: subjec-
tively (Am I sure that I am remembering and not imagining?) and objectively (Does my memory claim cohere with
other phenomena?)

As for the first sort of test, those who advance a
representative theory have often dealt with this question by suggesting that a memory presentation represents
a genuine memory when the presentation has certain peculiar qualities -- "memory indicators" of some sort.
Hume, for example, holds that

> 'Tis evident at first sight, that the
> ideas of memory are much more lively
> and strong than those of the imagina-
> tion, and that the former faculty
> paints its objects in more distinct
> colours, than any which are employed
> by the latter.[8]

As has been frequently pointed out, however, imagination
can generate lively and strong images as well. The
search for "memory indicators" has persisted, so that
we find Russell annexing a "feeling of familiarity" to
genuine memory claims so as to distinguish them from
imagination.[9]

Augustine recognizes a similar problem. Suppose
that x has been forgotten. According to Augustine I

consider various memories, u, v, w, etc., until I find
x. This procedure seems to entail that I have never
forgotten x, however. First, if I have utterly forgotten x, then I will not try to remember x. "For even
the thing we remember that we forgot, we had not
utterly forgotten. For if we had utterly forgotten it,
we should not even be able to think of looking for
it."[10]   Second, if we had truly forgotten x, we would
not be able to recognize x even if we do recall it.

> And if the memory chances to offer us
> something else instead, we reject it
> until we come upon the thing we are
> looking for. And when we come upon
> it we say: "This is it"; but we could
> not say this unless we recognized it,
> and we could not recognize it unless
> we remembered it. Yet certainly we
> had forgotten it.[11]

I think it helpful to consider just what situations
would require the presence of memory indicators. We
shall only search for (or require) a special indicator
of genuine memory for those cases in which there is
some question about a memory report (again, assuming
that the report is honest). Further, it will not be
enough for someone to simply deny my memory claim.
The memory claim will have to be denied for a reason,
whether the reason is someone else's memory, or a
newspaper report, or some other generally reputable
historical evidence which denies my memory claim.

In response to a denial of a memory claim, we
might examine the memory presentation again, but such
an examination will not satisfy the person who doubts
the report, and such an examination should not satisfy
the rememberer. It will not satisfy the person who
doubts the report because the first time the memory

report was made, and doubted, it was presumably made on grounds of the memory presentation. The reaffirmed report is made on the same grounds. "Looking again" will not satisfy someone who had reason to disbelieve the first report, since it was just the memory claim, based on the memory presentation, that was doubted. The person who makes the memory claim should not be satisfied with simply reexamining the claim because the claim was denied for specific reasons, and, if we assume that there are consequences to the claim, because it is important to establish its truth. Although subjective evidence (memory presentations) will do to make the initial memory claim, in face of denial, evidence to the contrary, etc., we must move from subjective tests to the second sort of test that may be applied to memories.

The external phenomena that support a memory claim include the memory reports of others, records in diaries, newspapers, photographs, footprints in snow, etc. Let us call these phenomena "generally reputable historical evidence." When phenomena of this sort cohere with my memory claim, then I say that my memory claim has been established. All this is to say that the characteristics that distinguish memory from imagination are of no use to us if they are subjective or internal or private in that they only make a difference (are convincing) when they are objective or external or public.

The ability to distinguish memory and imagination is taken to be crucial and central to any correct account of memory. We have seen that there are techniques for the verification of memory claims that may serve to separate imaginations from memories. These techniques may appeal to a correspondence between the evidence my memory supplies and the evidence that may

be supplied by other sources. There is, however, a
special case involving the possibility of confusing a
genuine memory and an imagination. What do we do when
we make a memory claim that is denied and there are no
other phenomena to support the claim?

Suppose that I am walking alone through a forest
and I see a rare bird. Upon encountering someone I report that I have seen a rare bird and I am doubted (the
bird should not be here at this time of year). How do
I establish that I have seen the bird? Generally, how
do I support a memory claim in the absence of other
generally reputable historical evidence?

The present problem is to distinguish between a
case in which I imagine that I have seen a bird and a
case in which I in fact remember that I have seen a
bird. However, we can see that the same problems that
hold for memory hold as well for acquisition. Imagine
that on my walk through the woods I carry a two-way
radio. I may report on the radio that I am seeing a
rare bird *as I see it*. In reply I might be asked how I
know that I am not imagining that I am seeing a bird.
If I am unable to capture the bird to show to the person who doubts me, and if there are no other people
around to see the bird so that my claim may be supported, I will then have nothing but my subjective reports to support my claim. If a report, whether about
a contemporary event or about a past event, is denied,
the means that I will use to verify my report will be
the same -- I shall appeal to other evidence, evidence
other than my subjective experiences.

When memories are called into question they may
be supported by what I have called generally reputable
historical evidence. When one or more of these sources
confirms my memory claim, the doubts about my claim
are to that degree vitiated.

Memory sceptics point out that generally reputable historical evidence is itself dependent upon my memory in some way. Photographs are generally reliable, but I know that photographs are generally reliable because I remember that photographs are generally reliable. The same observations may be made about my reliance on diaries, newspapers, and so on. I may rely on diaries because I remember that they are generally reliable records of past events; I may rely on newspapers for the same reason. I remember some other more fundamental things in order to rely upon these sources of information. I remember, for example, that since ink doesn't change its character over time, the letters I wrote last week are the same as the letters I read today.

All of these observations make scepticism regarding memory claims seem reasonable because they lead to the request that someone who wishes to justify memory as a source of knowledge about the past do so in a non-circular manner. One must provide a justification of memory which does not itself assume that memory is a reliable source of knowledge of the past.

I shall respond to this criticism in two general ways. First, I shall seriously entertain the sceptical hypothesis that is implicit in this criticism. Second, I shall argue that the target of this scepticism, if we take the scepticism seriously, is too narrow.

Taking the Sceptic Seriously

What are the consequences of seriously entertaining the hypothesis that the various sources of generally reputable historical evidence are equally unreliable? Let us examine a memory claim that I might make and, taking the sceptic seriously, consider how the sceptic might respond.

Suppose that I claim to remember meeting the Prince of Wales on a camping trip in British Columbia

in 1970. Someone might doubt my claim. In support I
might marshall the following experience: My friends,
x, y, and z, who accompanied me on that camping trip
all remember that they, too, met the Prince of Wales at
the time and at the place that I remember having met
him. My diary, and the diaries of x, y and z, all report the meeting with the Prince of Wales. Further,
the British Columbia newspapers, national news maga-
zines and the London newspapers all report that the
Prince of Wales was in British Columbia on the dates of
my camping trip and that he went on a camping trip into
the same forest that I report having camped in.

For some perverse reason this may not be enough to
convince someone that I met the Prince of Wales while I
was camping. Suppose that my attempt to support my
claim now becomes more vigorous. I travel to British
Columbia and interview various persons who were present
during the Prince's visit. Some of them report having
accompanied the Prince and they report that they remember meeting me, x, y, and z on the camping trip. Their
diaries report our meeting and, upon my request, they
obtain letters which they wrote to friends at the time
reporting our meeting. I travel to the sight of the
meeting in 1970 and there I discover the campground.
Through some fortuitous circumstances I am able to
trace the outline of my tent and of the campfire. I am
able to identify the trail that the Prince followed as
he came to the campsite. The evidence at the campsite
is consistent with my earlier reports. I find a cigarette lighter with the Prince's crest on it. I fly
to London to interview the Prince. He reports that he
remembers the meeting. He produces photographs of the
meeting showing himself, me, x, y, and z. I give him
his cigarette lighter and we both remember that he
lost it on his camping trip.

In light of all of this evidence, then, I am prepared to say that I remember having met the Prince of Wales under the circumstances described, and, further, to claim that my memory of the meeting is an accurate account of an historic event.

If we are to take the sceptic seriously, ruling out the possibility of a massive hoax (since in principle this sort of investigation could be performed for a large number of memory claims, we would have to suppose that any or all of those could or would be hoaxes) we would take the following line. All of the evidence presented in favor of my claim to have met the Prince of Wales in British Columbia in 1970 assumed that memory was accurate in one way or other. It is possible that all of the memories of all the witnesses to the event were faulty; it is possible that the newspapers' reports have all changed over time; it is possible that the photographs which the Prince produced have changed over time; it is possible that the campsite somehow changed and that the Prince's lighter was transported to the site by some means other than the Prince's hand. The sceptic asks us to seriously entertain the possibility that all this has happened. But, this isn't all that the sceptic asks. Remember that all of the generally reputable historical phenomena give a consistent report. Thus, the sceptic also asks that we entertain the possibility that all of this has happened in a consistent and coherent manner such that *all* of the diaries and *all* of the newspapers, memories, photographs, characteristics of the campsite, letters and so on have changed in exactly the same way.

The alternatives we face, then, are (a) my memory is generally reliable -- thus, since I remember that I met the Prince of Wales in British Columbia in 1970 (and since this memory coheres with other phenomena) I

can safely say that I met the Prince of Wales in 1970,
or (b) my memory cannot be relied upon to report anything about the past because any other evidence that I
might appeal to depends upon my remembering that it is
reliable evidence about the past. Therefore, I can't
be sure whether or not I have met the Prince of Wales.

Suppose that I decide to accept the second hypothesis. That is, suppose that I take seriously the sceptic's suggestion. I may now do one of two things,
depending upon whether or not I know (or can in some
way determine) that the various items that compose
generally reputable historical evidence have a nasty
habit of changing radically as they age.

If I know that these phenomena change over time,
then I may ask what sort of account of the world I can
produce that will explain all of these changes. In
other words, just what sort of world is the sceptic
suggesting? Presumably, if I know that generally reliable historical evidence changes over time, I may try
in some way to describe the change. This description
may take the form of principles or laws that relate how
memories, records, ink marks, footsteps in the snow,
geological faults, and so on all change in some coherent and consistent manner. These relations are going
to have to tie together psychological, physiological,
physical, chemical and biological phenomena and, as
well, are going to have to explain in some way or other
this unitary change. If such laws or principles could
be formulated, then it would seem plausible for someone to examine evidence about historic events in light
of such principles or laws with the aim of retracing
the coherent and consistent change that has occurred
in the evidence. In the process of retracing these
changes I would be learning about the past, so that the
evidence, changed though it may be, is nonetheless

evidence about the past. (In fact, general notions
about how substances and arrangements of material objects change over time are highly useful to archaeolo-
gists, anthropologists and geologists, among others,
when *they* consider evidence about the past.)

At first, the suggestion that we might know about
the changes in generally reputable historical evidence
seems peculiar. It seems to be contrary to the general
spirit of scepticism, which usually amounts to "How do
you know that some undetectable and misleading state of
affairs is not in fact the case?") However, unless the
changes that occur in records, newspapers, geological
faults and so on are consistent with certain generally
observable patterns (sociological or historical patterns, for example), it is going to be clear to people
that *something* has happened.

Here is an example of what I have in mind. Let us
suppose that history books have altered coherently and
consistently through time so that a study of history
will teach us that nations may violate the borders of
other nations with impunity. Our records tell us that
nations never react violently to a violation of their
borders. In light of this, we would undoubtedly be
surprised when a country responded to an invasion by
going to war. In other words, if we are unable to rely
upon the reports of generally reputable historical evidence we are thereby guaranteed a constant flow of surprises. These surprises, I suggest, would have to be
explained.

A position much closer to the spirit of scepticism
is to suppose that I do not know that all of the evidence about the past has undergone a unitary change --
that is, there are no surprises. We may ask what
difference these changes will make in our conceptual
scheme. Specifically, what impact will the changing of

all of these phenomena have upon our conception of the
past and upon our notion of history? Presumably, it
will have none. What we mean by the words "past" and
"history" may well be events that have occurred at some
time previous to this one, but the only evidence we
have for these events is generally reputable historical
evidence. Since the operational presence of the past,
then, is represented by generally reputable historical
evidence, the suggestion that this evidence has somehow
"changed" coherently and consistently over time, and
the consequent suggestion that the world has changed as
well, so that there are no surprises, would seem to be
of small moment.

Broadening the Target

There is a reply to this line of argument that we
might expect from a sceptic. That the consistent and
coherent change of generally reputable historical evidence is of no practical consequence is an absurd suggestion. It is quite simply a fact that were evidence
of some event at some moment T_1 to change by T_2, then
an observer present at T_1 would report something at T_1
that would be different from the report he (and all
evidence) would give at T_2. One "unimportant consequence" that follows from my suggestion, then, is the
abandonment of any claim that generally reputable historical evidence reports the truth.

There is a simple response to this. The assumption of the view of the memory sceptic, of course, is
that claims about the present have special epistemological status, so that claims about the past somehow
have to meet the requirement of being consistent with
claims about the present. In fact (by the sceptical
hypothesis), changed or not, they do. Further, if we
are to take seriously the sceptic's charge about the
reliability of evidence about the past, we might just

as well question the reliability of evidence about the
present.

Let us return to the original question. Do we
maintain the view that memory is generally a reliable
source of information about the past, or do we reject
memory because of possible errors? In order to convince us of the unreliability of memory, the sceptic
will have to advance an enormously complex hypothesis
which will delineate the various ways in which psychological, physical, chemical, and other phenomena are
interrelated so as to change coherently and consistently over time. The alternative hypothesis, that the
world is as it seems to be, more or less, is simpler
and explains the same phenomena.

Augustine and Memory

What of the role that memory plays in Augustine's
epistemology? The suggestion central to the preceding
line of argument is that memory has a certain utility
in every day affairs. To undermine memory is to undermine these garden-variety experiences. Augustine recognizes this utility. "...{F}rom these {the things I
remember} again I can picture actions and events and
hopes for the future, and upon them all I can meditate
as if they were present. 'I shall do this or that', I
say to myself..."[12]   No matter what I do, my action
"...must be accompanied once by the expectation that it
can be completed and also by memory, in order to com-
prehend the measure of its capacity."[13]   Augustine is
suggesting that we deal with the future by drawing in-
ductions from past experience. However, he does not
accept induction as a basis for knowledge uncritically.
"We do not conjecture the past from the future, but the
future from the past, yet not with a sure knowledge."[14]

III

In his excellent *The Christian Philosophy of St.
Augustine*, Professor Gilson contrasts Augustine's

account of knowledge as a kind of remembering with the
Platonic doctrine of reminiscence. He tells us that
"The Platonic recollection of the past gives way to
that Augustinian memory of the present whose role becomes more and more important."[15]   Memory of the *present*? It seems peculiar to speak of remembering the
present and it is just this sort of peculiarity that
seems to support the view that Augustine means more
than "memory" when he uses *memoria*.

When I discussed the way in which we can support
our memory claims through appeal to generally reputable
evidence I pointed out that such support is often ruled
out since it depends upon the assumption that memory is
accurate. I suggested that if this criticism is taken
seriously, then nothing whatever can count as knowledge,
even acquired knowledge -- that in fact the memory
sceptic chooses too narrow a target, since we can know
nothing at all if memory is not reliable.

Many philosophers have held for various reasons
that memory is essential to any sort of knowledge.

> And we in our thoughts, reasonings,
> and knowledge could not proceed be-
> yond present objects, were it not
> for the assistance of our memories;
> wherein there may be two defects:
>
> First, that it loses the idea
> quite, and so far it produces per-
> fect ignorance. For since we can
> know nothing further than we have
> the idea of it, when that is gone
> we are in perfect ignorance.[16]

"...{T}he assumption {that memory is generally reli-
able} is reasonable, at least in that it has to be
made if knowledge is ever to be possible at all."[17]
Augustine shares this insight.

An explicit discussion of the importance of memory for the acquisition of knowledge may be found in Augustine's *De Trinitate*.[18] Often we try to ignore physical hardship,

> ...{T}he will turns away the memory
> from the sense when it is intent on
> something else, and does not allow
> things that are present to cling to
> it...when someone is speaking to us
> and we are thinking of something
> else, it often appears as if we had
> not heard him...we did hear, but we
> did not remember...[19]

We don't know what the speaker said because "...the will...is wont to fix them {the words} in memory."[20] Memory is essential to understanding any and every experience. "...{A}s the limit of perceiving is in bodies, so the limit of thinking is in memory."[21]

Augustine's view that all knowledge claims are grounded in memory seems readily defensible. If I know P, then I have either just acquired P, or I remember P. Imagine someone who suffers from a peculiar malady. He instantly forgets everything he acquires. (One may well wonder whether "forgets" is the correct word. If the concept of forgetting entails having once known or learned, then this instant amnesiac isn't really forgetting.) Let us call this poor fellow Ian. Now, if *P* is something which Ian is told or experiences, it seems that Ian could never know anything.

Consider mediate acquisition, a report that someone might be making to Ian: "The paper is white." If Ian did not remember the meanings of words, he would never be able to understand the report. Further, if this report were made to Ian he would only be aware of each discrete sound as it occurred, having forgotten

the immediately previous sound. He would have
forgotten the sounds made at the beginning of the sentence by the time the sentence ended. On just about
any view of language, a central problem of meaning is
how one is able to get some understanding of what a
speaker intends simply on the basis of a series of
sounds which the speaker makes. For Ian there would be
no series of sounds, only individual sounds which he
could not remember even if they mean anything, since he
would not remember their meanings.

> ...{T}he only reason why I could
> understand what the narrator was
> saying, even though I then heard
> his words put together for the
> first time in a connected dis-
> course, was because I remembered
> generically the individual things
> that he described.[22]

Consider immediate acquisition. In the case of
perception (where "perception" may be taken very
broadly, as for example, what a dog does when it walks
around a tree), it is difficult to conjure up a case.
A tree is in Ian's environment. Is Ian aware of the
tree's presence? By observing Ian, what sort of evidence could we gain that Ian was aware of the tree's
presence? Let us suppose (I think, contrary to the
hypothesis) that Ian is able to walk. He walks toward the tree. One bit of evidence that would be sufficient for us to say, "Ian did not see the tree,"
would be his walking into the tree. Even if we held
that Ian could be "aware" of the tree's presence mo-
mentarily, this awareness would never be translatable
into action. Avoiding the tree would require remembering the principle of impenetrability, applying that
principle to the present case, and remembering how to

avoid trees. Ian would walk into the tree. Whether
one advances a causal account of perception or a phenomenalism, some sort of inferences must be drawn and
inferences take time and memory.

We shall consider Augustine's account of perception in the next chapter. The five well-known messengers of the body send a message to the mind where an
image is constructed. In order to construct the image
the mind has to remember the message. Thus since, for
Augustine, perception is a kind of report, memory is
essential for perception.

So, as it is for us, memory for Augustine is crucial to any knowledge. In fact, there is good evidence
that Augustine's analysis of memory leads him to con-
clude with Norman Malcolm that: "A being without factual memory would have no mental powers to speak of,
and he would not readily be a man even if he had the
human form."[23] For Augustine identifies memory with
the ego. "Great is the power of memory...and this
thing is my mind, this thing am I."[24]

If all knowledge involves memory, what are we now
to make of Professor Matthews' claim that for
Augustine "...whenever we are asked about familiar, but
absent, sensible things we respond by changing the subject..."[25] For Augustine, knowledge claims about material objects are, like knowledge claims generally,
essentially inner. They take as objects images. Thus,
Professor Matthews might well say that for Augustine
whenever one talks about material objects, whether
present or absent, one changes the subject for,

> ...what a body in a particular place
> is to the sense of the body, that the
> likeness of the body in the memory is
> to the eye of the mind; and what the
> vision of one seeing is to that species

> of the body from which the sense
> is informed, that the vision of
> one thinking is to the image of
> the body that is fixed in the
> memory, from which the eye of
> the mind is informed...[26]

This point is not a trivial one. The context of *De Magistro* from which Professor Matthews quotes the offending passage is an explanation of learning. Augustine explains to Adeodatus that, appearances to the contrary, we never learn from things nor do we learn from people. The process of "learning" is irreducibly inner. If this is the view that Augustine is suggesting here, then it should not be surprising that for him all knowledge claims are about mental images rather than about things themselves.

Just what question about memory claims is Augustine concerned to answer? I see no reason to suppose that in this context Augustine is trying to argue in favor of memory as being a good source of our knowledge of the past, or for our knowledge of absent material objects. His concern is a fundamental one. The passages quoted by Matthews appear between two sections of *De Magistro*. The earlier section is concerned to explain how it is that we make claims about present material objects. The latter section explains how we can make knowledge claims about eternal truths. One peculiarity of knowledge claims other than those grounded in memory is that *something* is immediate to the claim -- either the presence of a corporeal object, or an eternal truth. I think that Augustine is trying to show that something is immediate to a knowledge claim about absent material objects as well, noting with Russell that, "...everything constituting a memory belief is happening *now*..."[27] But, what is it that

is immediate to one who is making a claim about an
absent material object? Not the object, by hypothesis,
but an image of an object. So, when we talk about an
absent object in *this* sense we talk about an image, and
how we would confirm or disconfirm such talk is irrelevant.

There is a final point to be made. We shall consider Augustine's account of communication in detail in
Chapter 7. However, here I must respond to the claim
that reports about absent material objects, since they
are about images, are reports that "change the subject."

It is important to get clear the way in which a
mental image and a word of inner-speech are related for
Augustine, and how a word of inner-speech is related to
a public utterance. There are passages in Augustine's
work in which mental images and inner-words are treated
as being identical. Augustine has visited Carthage and
he thus has an image of Carthage stored in his memory.
If he wants to think of Carthage he first searches his
memory until he finds his image of that city.

> For its image in my mind is its word,
> not that sound of three syllables
> when Carthage is named {Carthago}, or
> even when that name itself is silently
> thought of during some period of time,
> but the word that I see in my mind
> when I utter this word of three syl-
> lables with my voice, or even before
> I utter it. [28]

Here Augustine indicates that the inner-word for
Carthage and the image of Carthage come to the same
thing. A public word has its meaning as a consequence
of its relationship to a private, inner-word. When we
speak we "bring forth" these private, inner-words
which reflect the properties of images. Thus, when

one speaks of a material object, whether that object is present or it is absent, one's speech is itself immediately generated by an image in spiritual vision. By treating inner-words and images in this way, Augustine is able to enjoy an important dividend of his inner-man locutions. When he wants to talk about what it is that he remembers when he remembers Carthage, he may speak of a mental image. This helps him to explain how he is able to remember what he remembers about Carthage (that it is dirty, that it is busy, that it is filled with Carthaginians, that it must be destroyed). On the other hand, when he wants to explain how it is that he is able to *tell* someone else about Carthage, he may appeal to his memory of Carthage as being an inner-word which may be brought forth as an outer-word.

When we want to tell someone something we know we express an inner-word of thought as a public utterance. "...{T}he word which sounds without is a sign of the word that shines within..."[29] The inner-word doesn't *become* a public utterance, it assumes an articulate sound. Thus, the inner-word is not changed. Rather, the inner-word seems to be a kind of cue to the production of an outer-word.[30] Augustine is not suggesting that one changes the subject when talking about absent objects; he is, instead, providing his account of how such talk can be meaningful.

IV

There are several characteristics of Augustine's epistemology that begin to emerge at this point. First, Augustine's account of knowledge is, at base, rational. Augustine is not suggesting a magic access to the sources of knowledge of the past. Rather, what we know of the past seems to be a consequence of fitting together an accurate representation of events.

Second, this fitting together is a creative act. Memory is not something that just happens; it requires

a deliberate effort on the part of the rememberer.
This is especially true when a memory claim must be
justified through appeal to other phenomena.

Third, the usefulness of Augustine's interiority
can be seen in the various aspects of his theory about
memory. The process of remembering is one that occurs
exclusively in the inner-man's domain.

Finally, the central difficulty for any study of
Augustine's epistemology becomes clear as we consider
memory. The individual elements of his epistemology
are interdependent to a degree that requires at least a
mention of all of them in a discussion of any one of
them. These characteristics will be seen in every aspect of Augustine's theory of knowledge.

Chapter 4

Footnotes

[1]
*Nam cum recordor patrem meum, id utique recordor
quod me deseruit, et nunc non est; cum autem
Carthaginem id quod est, et quod ipse deserui.
Epistola* (hereafter EP) 7, 1.

[2]
*...non posse in memoriam venire, nisi viso illo
imaginario.*   EP 7, 1.

[3]
*Ibi reconditum est quidquid etiam cogitamus, vel
augendo vel minuendo, vel utcumque variando ea quae
sensus attigerit; et si quid aliud commendatum et
repositum est, quod nondum absorbuit et sepelivit
oblivio.   Ibi quando sum, posco ut proferatur quidquid
volo, et quaedam statim prodeunt; quaedam requiruntur
diutius, et tanquam de abstrusioribus quibusdam
receptaculis eruuntur; quaedam catervatim se proruunt,
et dum aliud petitur et quaeritur, prosiliunt in medium
quasi dicentia.   Ne forte nos sumus?   Et abigo ea manu
cordis a facie recordationis meae, donec anubiletur
quod volo, atque in conspectum prodeat ex abditis.*
CO X, 8, 12.

[4]
...corporis similitudine quam memoria tenet...
DT XI, 3, 6.

[5]
Gareth B. Matthews, "Augustine on Speaking from
Memory," *American Philosophical Quarterly*, Vol. 2,
No. 2, p. 1.

[6]
*Cum vero non de iis quae coram sentimus, sed de
his quae aliquando sensimus quaeritur; non jam res
ipsas, sed imagines ab iis impressas memoriaeque
mandatas loquimur...*   DMA 12, 39.

[7]
Matthews, "Memory," p. 4.

[8]
David Hume, *A Treatise of Human Nature*, ed. L.A.
Selby-Bigge, Oxford, 1968, p. 9.

[9]
Bertrand Russell, *Analysis of Mind*, George Allen and Unwin, 1921, p. 161.

[10]
Neque enim omni modo adhuc obliti sumus, quod vel oblitos nos esse meminimus. Hoc ergo nec amissum quaerere poterimus, quod omnino obliti fuerimus. CO X, 19.

[11]
Et ibi si aliud pro alio forte offeratur, respuimus, donec illud occurat quod quaerimus. Et cum occurit, dicimus: "Hoc est"; quod non diceremus, nisi agnosceremus, nec agnosceremus, nisi meminissemus. Certe enim obliti fueramus. CO X, 19.

[12]
...atque ex his etiam futuras actiones et eventa et spes, et haec omnia rurus quasi praesentia meditor. "Faciam hoc et illud" dico apud me... CO X, 8.

[13]
Porro quod sic agitur, et exspectatione opus est ut peragi, et memoria ut comprehendi queat quantum potest. DIA 3, 3.

[14]
Nec ex futuris praeterita, sed futura ex praeteritis, non tamen firma cognitione conjicimus. DT XV, 7, 13.

[15]
Etienne Gilson, *The Christian Philosophy of Saint Augustine*, tr. L.E.M. Lynch, Random House, 1960, p. 75.

[16]
John Locke, *An Essay Concerning Human Understanding* II, 10, 8.

[17]
Don Locke, *Memory*, Doubleday-Anchor (Garden City, N.Y., 1971), p. 135.

[18]
DT XI, 8.

[19]
Memoriam vero a sensu voluntas avertit, cum in aliud intenta non ei sinit inhaerere praesentia... Cum saepe coram loquentem nobis aliquem aliud cogitando non audisse nobis videmur...audimus enim, sed non meminimus... DT XI, 8, 15.

[20]
...*voluntatis, per quem solent infigi memoriae.*
DT XI, 8, 15.

[21]
...*sicut in corporibus sentiendi, sic in memoria
est cogitandi modus.* DT XI, 8, 14.

[22]
*Neque enim vel intelligere possem narrantem, si
ea quae dicit, et se contexta tunc primum audirem, non
tamen generaliter singula meminissem.* DT XI, 8, 14.

[23]
Norman Malcolm, "Three Forms of Memory,"
Knowledge and Certainty, Prentice-Hall, 1965, p. 212.

[24]
*Magna vis est memoriae...et hoc animus est, et hoc
ego ipse sum.* CO X, 17.

[25]
Matthews, "Memory," p. 157.

[26]
*Quod ergo est ad corporis sensum aliquod corpus in
loco; hoc est ad animi aciem similitudo corporis in
memoria: et quod est aspicientis visio ad eam speciem
corporis ex qua sensus formatur; hoc est visio
cogitantis ad imaginem corporis in memoria constitutam
ex qua formatur acies animi...* DT XI, 4, 7.

[27]
Russell, *Analysis*, p. 159.

[28]
*Ipsa enim phantasia ejus in memoria mea verbum
ejus, non sonus iste trisyllabus cum Carthago nominatur,
vel etiam tacite nomen ipsum per spatia-temporum
cogitatur; sed illud quod in animo meo cerno, cum hoc
trisyllabum voce profero, vel antequam proferam.* DT
VIII, 6, 9.

[29]
*Prointe verbum quod foris sonat, signum est verbi
quod intus lucet...* DT XV, 11, 20.

[30]
See SE 187, 3.

CHAPTER 5

PERCEPTION

Visio Spiritualis

There is some question about whether Augustine is
concerned with knowledge of the physical world. Some
commentators have argued that knowledge of the material
world is unimportant for Augustine. They have based
this view on two characteristics of his comments on
knowledge. First, his frequently occurring assertion
that sensation is not knowledge. Second, his equally
frequent assertion that the important objects of knowledge are only found within us. Thus, it is said, for
Augustine the material world is taken to be at best
irrelevant -- at worst a distraction -- for the putative knower. These emphases in Augustine's writing
have been given as the reason for his allegedly inadequate analysis of knowledge of the material world.
This treatment of Augustine is, I think, misleading.

I

Augustine maintains that sensation is not knowledge.[1] It is not knowledge because sensation is uninterpreted experience. Only when sensation is ordered
does it become knowledge. The mind is the ordering
agency; thus, we only know about the external world
when the mind actively orders experience. When
wishing to know anything, Augustine urges a turning inward. This is because even knowledge of the outer

world results only from the functioning of inner
faculties.

I am, of course, not denying that for Augustine
the real sources of wisdom are purely inner. Nor am I
ignoring his frequent assertion that the senses can be
distracting and misleading.[2] What I am maintaining is
that the inward-turning character of Augustine's epistemology ought not to be taken as indicating a dis-
regard for knowledge of the material world, since any
sort of knowledge requires such an inward turning.

On the positive side, there are clearly places in
which Augustine recognized the importance of perception.

> ...knowledge of truth, gleaned by
> intelligence and reasoning, is in-
> deed slender because of the corrupt-
> ible body weighing down the soul.
> As St. Paul says, 'We know in part'.
> Still, this knowledge is certain.
> Believers, moreover, trust the
> report of the bodily senses which
> subserve the intelligence. If they
> are at times deceived, they are at
> least better off than those who
> maintain that the senses can never
> be trusted.[3]

Not only is such knowledge possible, it is also useful.

> The quality of sensation enables one
> according to his capacity to perceive
> the truth in corporeal things corre-
> sponding to their mode and nature,
> and to distinguish more or less ac-
> curately the true from the false.
> The usefulness of sensation enables
> us to judge things by way of approval

> or disapproval, acceptance or rejection,
> seeking or avoidance, in reference to
> our way of life.[4]

Finally, having established the central importance of
memory for his epistemology in the previous chapter, it
is important to note that Augustine held memory to be
limited by perception.[5]

Augustine may well have thought that knowledge of
the physical world is of secondary importance, but this
does not mean that he thought it unimportant. An examination of his theory of perception demonstrates that
he thought knowledge of the physical world worthy of
attention.

II

Approaching the Problem

A philosopher's manner of dealing with the problem
of perception is tempered by the path that leads him to
that problem. There are several paths. One can see
perception as a problem for explaining a physical relationship, determining how the sense organs interact
with the physical world to produce non-physical sensations. One can see a theory of perception as a means
of closing the appearance-reality gap, taking such a
theory to account for how the testimony of the senses
provides evidence about an objective, external reality.
One can also see the problem of perception to be the
center of another problem: the unification of diverse
aspects in an ontology.

Although Augustine considers the physiological
problems of perception (at, for example, *De Genesi ad
Litteram* and *De Anima et ejus Origine*), I am concerned
in this chapter with the latter two problems mentioned
above. The key to understanding Augustine's treatment
of perception is to be found in his ontology and his
consideration of the problem of appearance and reality.

Augustine was aware of the classical problem of
appearance and reality. That problem may be stated
simply as follows: Human beings have immediate access
only to mental phenomena. Among these mental phenomena
are sensations. We take some of these sensations to be
evidence for non-mental phenomena. Why should certain
of our sensations serve as evidence for an objective
mind-independent reality? The problem becomes a problem, of course, because of the experience of error. We
rely upon appearance -- upon the way the world seems to
us -- for our understanding of reality -- our understanding of how the world "really" is. But sometimes
we make mistakes in moving from appearance to reality.
Sceptics point to the phenomenon of error in an attempt
to undermine our reliance upon the appearance/reality
connection. Augustine states this sceptical problem in
De Trinitate, book XV.[6] In response to the scepticism
of the academics he advances his *Si fallor, sum* argument, which we considered in Chapter 2. In presenting
that argument, he indicates that he does not wish to
consider knowledge of the physical world, because such
knowledge is gained by means of the body's senses, and
in the case of sense knowledge "...so many things are
different from what they seem."[7] Augustine, then, is
aware of the problem of appearance and reality but it
is not the only road he follows to an analysis of perception.

The other path may be seen in terms of a difficulty in Augustine's ontology, a difficulty he may
have inherited from Plotinus. It is a principle that
most commentators on Augustine's epistemology encounter, note and surrender to. It seems to render
Augustine's theory of perception untenable.

Augustine maintains, first, that there is a hierarchy in the universe and, second, that within this

hierarchy an inferior thing cannot bring about change
in a superior thing.[8] He confronts this problem in *De
Musica* "...you should think it strange that the body
can affect something in the soul."[9] He describes as
"disturbing" the manner in which "...the sounding numbers (i.e., noises) which are certainly material or in
a body in some sense, are to be taken as superior to
those (numbers) which are found in the soul when we
sense."[10] Since material things cannot bring about
change in human minds, it is difficult to demonstrate
how we come to know about our physical environment.
Usually Augustine's doctrine of "vital attention" is
taken to provide him with an account of perception.[11]
The problem is that those who utilize vital attention
in this way do not work out the details of Augustine's
doctrine. Usually, this failure to provide a complete
analysis is justified on the grounds that Augustine
himself gives knowledge gained through the senses a
secondary importance in his epistemology. The primary
focus of human knowledge is upon eternal truths. However, Augustine thinks that knowledge of the physical
world is important. Further, he does discuss several
different kinds of knowledge of the corporeal world.
We can judge whether or not an object is beautiful or
just, we can discuss objects that are present to us,
objects we have seen in the past, and objects that are
described to us by others.[12] It is in his discussion
of knowledge in these latter senses that Augustine develops epistemological principles that provide the
basis for his treatment of knowledge of the physical
world and, in important respects, anticipate later
epistemological theories.

In a letter to Consentius, written about 410,
Augustine explains that

> ...there are three sorts of things
> that are seen: a class of bodily
> things...a class of things that are
> similar to bodies...and a third
> class, which is distinct from the
> other two in that none of it (no
> member of it) is a body, nor has[13]
> any likeness to a body...

In Book XII of his *De Genesi ad Litteram* Augustine discusses three sorts of visions which he uses to explain
how we see the three sorts of things that can be seen.
These three visions are called by Augustine *visio
corporis*, *visio spiritualis* and *visio intellectus*. I
shall use the following terminology: for *visio
corporis* I shall use "Bodily sight," for *visio
spiritualis* either "animal sight" or "spiritual vision"
(context and function will determine which term I use,
as shall be explained below), for *visio intellectus*
"Intellectual vision."

Visio Corporis

      Augustine's discussion of bodily sight is not re-
stricted to those sensations annexed to the bodily eyes
but may be seen as a discussion of any and all of the
"...five well-known messengers of the body";[14] in effect, he uses "bodily sight" as a general term for
bodily sensation. There are two useful explanations
for his so treating bodily sight.

      First, Augustine (as have many philosophers) is
focusing upon one of the senses as an heuristic device
for all of the senses. "When I speak of sight," he
might say, "Substitute 'hearing', 'taste', and so on
where appropriate." In this context "sight" is a convenient shorthand for any of the five senses.

      Second, Augustine literally takes each of the
body's senses to be associated with bodily sight, so

that hearing *is* bodily sight, as is tasting, smelling,
etc. Augustine holds that "...bodily sensation belongs
to the visible, corporeal world..."[15] Light, the
finest of all the elements in corporeal things, is dif-
fused by and shines from the eyes, whereupon it inter-
mingles with material objects to bring about all of the
bodily sensations. Thus, it is proper to refer to each
of the bodily senses as "bodily sight."

The objects of bodily sight are material objects
and everything that can be known about material objects.[16] However, bodily sight is not our source of
knowledge about corporeal things.[17] In order to determine how Augustine accounts for our knowledge of the
material world we must follow the messages sent by the
messengers of the soul to the second sort of vision
that he discusses. "...all of the senses of the body
bring intelligence to the heart within of what they
have perceived abroad..."[18] This second sort of
vision is *visio spiritualis*.

Visio Spiritualis

There are three related problems concerning
Augustine's discussion of *visio spiritualis*. First, we
must decide how to translate the phrase. Second, we
must determine whether *visio spiritualis* is an inner
faculty or an outer faculty for Augustine. Third, we
must decide what role *visio spiritualis* plays in
Augustine's epistemology.

As for the difficulty in translation, the practice
seems to be to translate *visio spiritualis* as "spiritual vision." But, *visio spiritualis* is not a sort of
vision peculiar to spiritual things, for Augustine
holds that animals as well as men have *visio spiritualis*; *visio spiritualis* is peculiar to things that
breathe. (I must confess I am tempted to translate

this as "pneumovision." However, *ipsa vocabuli
novitate nimis absurdum est ut dicamus*.) I shall use
two terms to refer to *visio spiritualis*. Generally, I
shall use "animal sight," sight of animated things. In
certain contexts, where, for example, Augustine is concerned to explain the sense in which *visio spiritualis*
is *spiritualis* I shall render it as "spiritual vision."
This may seem to be playing a loose game. It will become clear below, however, that Augustine's discussion
of *visio spiritualis* is one of his most elusive, and
that he seems to have two separate and distinct uses
for the term. In working out these uses I shall justify the translations.

The second difficulty in Augustine's discussion of
visio spiritualis consists in determining whether he
thought this sort of vision was an inner or an outer
faculty; that is, whether he thought it to be a function of the mind or of the body. I shall argue that he
takes it to be one or the other, depending upon the
context of his discussion.

Visio spiritualis as an outer faculty -- "animal
sight": There are contexts in which Augustine indicates that the functioning of animal sight is not a
sufficient condition for the inner-man's learning
about the corporeal world. Sometimes animal sight
functions unheeded. Consider the experience of looking
without seeing. I walk along a road looking ahead.
Approaching is someone I know. I move aside as we pass
and he greets me. Suddenly, I recognize him.
Augustine treats this issue in *De Quantitate Animae*.
We look in order to see and seeing is valued more
highly than looking. "...looking is one thing, seeing
another..."[19]   Both animals and men deal with the corporeal world by means of the animal sight, but when

animal sight functions in this mode it is not a source
of knowledge. Augustine draws the distinction between
looking and seeing in order to demonstrate that animals
do not have true knowledge. He explains the use of
animal sight by beasts in mechanistic terms.

> As a matter of fact, many brute animals
> have keener sense-perception than we
> have... In mind and reason and knowl-
> edge we have been placed over them by
> God. The sense faculty they have, con-
> joined with the powerful force of habit,
> is able to discern the things that bring
> pleasure to souls such as theirs. Be-
> sides, this happens all the more easily
> because the soul of brute animals is more
> closely bound to the body; and it is to
> the latter that the senses belong which
> the soul uses for the life and enjoyment
> it derives from that same body.[20]

What animals do with animal sight parallels a man's
stepping aside unconsciously for an obstacle. The
problem is that people are able to know about the corporeal world presented by animal sight, but it seems
that for Augustine nothing can be known solely *via* the
animal sight. Augustine tells us that

> ...signs of things are formed in the mind
> and that an understanding of the signs
> shines forth in the mind. According to
> this distinction, then, I have designated
> as spiritual the kind of vision by which
> we represent in thought the images of
> bodies, even in their absence.[21]

Humans have a capacity that animals lack: they can
learn things through the images reported by animal
sight.

For Augustine images are not only of material
objects that are present. They can be of absent material objects as well. In the case of material objects
that are present, at exactly the moment that we encounter material objects with the bodily sight an image appears in the animal sight which resembles the object or
objects perceived by the bodily sight. In the case of
absent material objects, the image generated in animal
sight is what Augustine calls a "true image," by which
he means an image of something that I have actually
seen in the past. On the other hand, the image may
also be a "fictitious" one, "...fashioned by the power
of thought..."[22]   As an example of these sorts of image
Augustine tells us that his "...manner of thinking of
Carthage, which (he knows) is different from (his) manner of thinking of Alexandria, which (he) does not
know."[23]   Whether Augustine is using animal sight to explain how we know anything about the material world, or
he is using it to explain memory, animal sight is always clearly imaginal.

I have already discussed the problem that *we*
might have in deciding how to translate *visio spiritualis*. Augustine recognized a different problem. He
does not intend for the sense in which *visio spiritualis* is *spiritualis* to be taken loosely.

Augustine takes his meaning of "spiritual"
            ...from that singular use of the word,
            found in the letter to the Corinthians,
            in which spirit is obviously distin-
            guished from mind. "For," says the
            apostle, "if I pray in a tongue my
            spirit prays but my understanding is
            unfruitful."[24]

Paul uses the word *lingua*, says Augustine, to describe
"...obscure and mystical signs which profit no man if

the understanding of the mind is removed from them, for
he hears what he does not understand."[25]   The Latin
lingua is similar to the English "tongue" in that it
can mean either a physical tongue or a language.
Clearly, Augustine takes Paul to mean by *lingua* a language that has certain unique properties. It is composed of signs, but these signs are peculiar in that
one requires a special comprehension in order to understand them, even when one is producing these signs.

Augustine claims that Paul is using a metaphor
(*verba translata*), the peculiarity of this use of
lingua being that it refers to a production of signs
before the producer understands what the signs mean.
Indeed, it is presumably possible (in fact, I think it
likely) to speak in *lingua* without ever understanding
the sense of the signs. What is required is a special
intuition of the mind before they are understood.

Although couched in terms of the somewhat fuzzy
doctrine of speaking in tongues, I do not think that
there is any special mystery about what Augustine has
in mind here. When one produces or hears *lingua* without comprehension, one's animal sight alone attends to
the image representing the corporeal world. There is
no understanding. Whatever animal sight is, its functioning is not a sufficient condition for knowledge.
In Augustine's theory more is required.

III

Perception as Representation

Many philosophers have advanced a representative
account of perception -- an account of perception that
requires a mental object of some sort (usually an
image) that serves as an intermediary. This intermediary serves as a medium for knowledge of the physical
object -- it transmits information about that object

by representing it.   Representative accounts
encounter difficulties.   One problem, recognized by
Augustine, is generated by the difficulty of distinguishing the object of the perception from whatever it
is that the perceiver is aware of when he perceives the
object.   There are two ways that this problem may be
understood.   The first is a contemporary problem,
usually characterized as the problem of appearance and
reality.   We have already encountered this problem in
other contexts, but in the present context it is not a
problem for Augustine, for he does not doubt the existence of material objects.   Thus, although it may turn
out that it makes no systematic difference for our
understanding of Augustine whether he thought that we
perceive material objects or images, it will not be because Augustine himself could feel comfortable with a
solipsistic phenomenalism.   For Augustine there *are*
material objects; it is important for his ontology that
such objects exist.   He is not satisfied merely to be
able to talk as *though* there were such objects.   So,
Augustine is not concerned with demonstrating that
images are evidence for physical objects.   What he does
is to argue that they are *representations* of physical
objects.

At *De Trinitate* XI, 9,16 Augustine outlines the
steps (images or forms or *species*) that relate material
objects to thoughts about material objects.

> ...the species of the body, which is
> perceived, produces the species which
> arises in the sense of the percipient;
> this latter gives rise to the species
> in the memory; finally, the species in
> the memory produces the species which
> arises in the gaze of thought.[26]

First, there is the material object, which itself has a
form. The form of the material object generates the
second form, a likeness or image in the bodily sight.
This image in the bodily sight, in turn, leads to the
third image -- the image (or phantasy) which is produced in memory. Finally, the image in memory leads to
the image in the gaze of thought. Since the bodily
sight does not produce images, and since the animal
sight generates images in memory, it would seem that
the two intermediate images or forms occur in the animal sight.

   Augustine's account commits him to the view that
there are four distinct forms present when a material
object is perceived. If his point in the passages in
De Trinitate is that in practice we do not distinguish
four different images or forms when we see material objects, then the question of whether or not, when we see
an object, what we see is the object itself or an image
which represents the object, becomes of secondary importance. Nothing of consequence for Augustine's attempt to explain inner phenomena depends upon our
deciding between objects and images as the objects of
inner sight when *visio spiritualis* is treated as animal
sight, an outer faculty. However, the question becomes
important when we treat *visio spiritualis* as an inner
faculty.

The Role of Visio Spiritualis

   It is fairly clear that for Augustine perceiving a
material object involves two elements, the material object itself and an image that the perceiver produces
internally. Augustine realizes that since we are only
aware of one of these elements there is scepticism regarding the existence of both of them. This scepticism
results from a failure to understand how an image is

related to the object which is imaged.[27]   Through an
ingenious argument by analogy, Augustine explains both
the relationship and why the relationship is puzzling.
There are two kinds of material substance that can hold
imprints or impressions formed by harder materials.
Some substances are able to hold an impression after
the object which causes the impression has been removed (think of a ring impressed in a cake of wax).
Others lose the impressions when the object causing the
impression is removed (think of a ring immersed in
water). If one takes the relationship between material
object and image to be analogous to a ring's being impressed in wax, then one will naturally be suspicious
of an account of perception which posits images *in addition to* material objects. Since the image vanishes
when the object is taken away (or, at least, since we
are no longer aware of the image when the object is removed), there seems no reason to suppose that the image
was ever there in the first place.

Augustine, of course, suggests that the model for
the relationship between material object and image is a
ring immersed in water. So long as the material object
is present the image is present. The fact that the
image vanishes when the object is no longer present to
the bodily senses is not a reason to suppose that it
was never there, any more than the water's not being
displaced now entails that it never was displaced.

In determining how *visio spiritualis* does what
Augustine would have it do we encounter a problem that
I mentioned earlier in this chapter. Augustine's
three visions are included in the hierarchy of the
created universe. Animal sight is superior to bodily
sight. Animal sight is not the sole source of any
knowledge. Bodily sight does not cause the image that

animal sight generates. How, then, is the mind informed
about what the bodily sight reports? How does *visio
spiritualis* know what image it is to create so that it
may report to intellectual vision something about the
corporeal world?

It is tempting to answer these questions by treating Augustine's theory as a causal, representative view
of perception. But such an account will not work because it would require that an inferior thing (a material object) bring about change in an ontologically
superior thing (a soul). Augustine maintains that the
body cannot construct anything spiritual.[28] Thus, it
is not the body that is responsible for the images that
represent the physical world. It is the inner-man who
produces the image. "...the sensation does not proceed
from that body which is seen, but from a living body
that perceives, to which the soul is fitted...yet the
vision is produced by the body that is seen."[29]

The problem for Augustine is not to be expressed,
then, in terms of how bodily sight generates a correct
image in animal sight, since bodily sight does not generate anything. Rather, the problem is, on one hand,
to explain how animal sight knows what image to create
so that it may report to intellectual vision something
about the corporeal world and, on the other hand, how
it is that intellectual vision knows what to do with
the image which is reported to it by animal sight.

Augustine deals with the problem of the source of
sensation in *De Musica* VI. This book of *De Musica* is
ostensibly a discussion of how one comes to recognize
the meter of St. Ambrose's hymn, "*Deus Creator
Omnium.*" In fact, the discussion is more important as
an explanation of the steps through which the uttered
verse is heard, thought, and then judged by one who is
listening to a reading of the hymn.

Augustine presents five stages (or separate operations) in the process from uttered noise to judged verse. (Because Augustine is explicating meter, and because verses are structured numerically, he calls these separate stages "numbers." I shall call them "stages.") They are: the voiced stage, the sounding stage, the noise stage (the noise that is heard by the audience), the remembered stage, and the discriminating stage.

The voiced stage is the production of the physical change which brings about a physical effect in the ears of the audience. We might here think of the operation of the reader's vocal chords. The sounding stage is the physical concussion of air that is produced by the voiced stage. The noise stage is the sound heard by the audience. Here again, to use a contemporary example, we might think of this as the vibration of the eardrums of the audience. No sense can be made of the verse as a verse -- as a meaningful or melodious series of noises -- unless the series is stored in memory. Thus, there is the remembered stage. Finally, when the audience judges whether the reciter has read well or poorly it judges at the discriminating stage. [30]

Augustine's analysis of a particular perceptual situation provides a context in which we can fairly easily isolate the problem at issue. The central problem for understanding Augustine's treatment of perception may be expressed in terms of the relationship among the sounding, noise and remembered stages. It is tempting to explain the noise and remembered stages as being effects for which the sounding stage is a cause. However, this explanation will not work because the sounding and noise stages are explicated in physical terms, while memory is explicated by appeal to a mind.

As we saw earlier, Augustine's ontology prohibits a
physical process from bringing about a change in a non-
physical thing. Augustine is able to solve this problem, but his solution to it, together with the theory
of knowledge of the material world that grows from that
solution, constitute the most elusive and difficult
elements of his epistemology.

Augustine's solution turns upon his notion that
the task of the soul -- of the inner-man -- is to maintain the life of the body. The inner-man "presides"
over the body. In one of his letters he says that the
interior eyes act as "...president of the tribunal..."[31]
This means that the inner-man is aware of the workings
of the body. This awareness is not a consequence of
the soul's passively receiving messages from the body's
senses, however. Augustine offers an active theory of
sensation. The inner-man is aware of events occurring
in the body by means of "a sort of vital attention."[32]
The inner-man *must* be aware of what is happening to the
body because without such awareness the body could suffer some dysfunction or could die.[33] When we experience a sensation we are experiencing the inner-man's
coming to know of a corporeal object or of some bodily
state.[34]

It is at this point that attempts to explicate
Augustine's account of perception break down. "The
inner-man presides over the body by means of vital attention," is a simple, compact phrase. In fact, it
has the ring of a slogan and, as with most slogans, it
conceals more than it reveals. The problem is to determine what this slogan means.

In *De Trinitate* XI, 2,3 Augustine presents his
analysis of the formation of images by the spiritual
vision. He draws a distinction between sense and

sensing and repeats the ontological principle that
sensation does not proceed from the object that is seen,
but he adds that "...the vision is produced by the body
that is seen."[35]   He is drawing a distinction between
sensations proceeding from something and sensations
being produced by something. Having the image *proceed*
from the physical object would, it seems, violate the
ontological hierarchy, but having the image produced by
the object does not. The difference between the two is
the difference between an unbroken series of physical
events and a series of events that is continued or modified by an agent. To say that the image proceeds from
the body would connect the image directly -- and exclusively -- to a physical process. But, Augustine's active theory of sensation is intended as an alternative
to such a series. The active theory requires the intervention of the perceiver. Thus,

>   ...the sense itself is informed by it
>   {the object which is sensed}, so that
>   it is no longer merely a sense...but
>   it is now also an informed sense which
>   is called vision. The vision, therefore,
>   is produced by the visible thing, but
>   not by it alone, unless the one who sees
>   is also present.[36]

What Augustine is *not* doing here is ruling out any role
at all for the material object in the production of the
mental image. What he does rule out is the operation
of the object *directly* on the body to produce the image.
It is necessary that both percipient and physical object interact.

>   ...vision is produced both by the
>   visible thing and the one who sees,
>   but in such a way that the sense of

> sight as well as the intention of
> seeing and beholding come from the
> one who sees, while that informing
> of the sense which is called vision,
> is imprinted by the body alone that
> is seen, namely, by some visible
> thing...[37]

What this rules out for Augustine is a simple look-and-
see model of perception -- a simple empiricism. But,
it does not rule out a role for the physical object in
perception. The troublesome relationship in *De Musica*
VI may be explained by maintaining that both the noise
stage and the remembered stage must interact before the
discriminatory stage may occur. This means that the
physical aspects of perception are not sufficient for
perception. "...we cannot indeed say that the physical
thing begets the sense, but it begets the form, as it
were, its own likeness, which arises in the sense when
we perceive anything by seeing."[38] The body is essential in producing the image which, "...arises in the
body and through the body in the soul, for it arises in
the sense, which is neither without the body nor without the soul."[39] However, "...the vision is not completely begotten by the form of the body alone, since
something else is applied to the body in order that it
may be formed by it, namely, the sense of the one who
sees."[40]

What is being ruled out by Augustine is the possibility that judgment (i.e., whatever occurs in the discriminatory stage) is caused solely by physical events.

Once the image has been formed, there is no longer
anything physical involved in perception.

> ...The place of that bodily species...
> is taken by the memory, retaining the

> species which the soul absorbs into
> itself through the bodily sense; and
> the vision, which was without when
> the sense was formed by a sensible
> body, is succeeded by a similar
> vision within, when the eye of the
> mind is formed from that which the
> memory retains and absent bodies are
> conceived...[41]

Augustine, then, is advancing a theory of perception that is non-mechanistic, non-empiricist and not purely phenomenalistic. The body *does* play a role in the production of the image in spiritual vision, but so does the mind. The mind's role is governed by the requirement that the images be formed in such a way as to guarantee the continuing survival of the body. This position is an unusual one in the history of epistemology, but it is by no means unique.

VI

If we view perception as an active tool, as a device *used* by human minds in order to create accurate representations of the external world, and if we see the motivation for the creation of such representations as being the survival of the human organism, then Augustine's account of perception ceases to be a mystery.

The argument for this position will require some preliminary groundwork that I will not claim to have been undertaken by Augustine. The position I shall describe below represents a "likely story." To put the point another way, had Augustine the advantage that we have of the philosophical developments of the last fifteen centuries, he would advance the following position.

We have seen that Augustine divides human beings
into two aspects -- the inner-man and the outer-man.
The inner-man is given many roles, but there is a particular task that concerns us here. The inner-man is
charged to preserve the outer-man. Thus, the physical
existence of the human organism is entrusted to the
inner-man. The inner-man may be seen as confronting
the undifferentiated, unstructured manifold of experience provided by the bodily senses. What we see is
"...a forest of things..."[42] Augustine must maintain
that these are the raw data with which the inner-man
deals, since he holds that the senses of the outer-man
report to the inner-man, *and* the outer-man is responsible for no knowledge. Were the experiences of the
outer-man structured in any way by the outer-man, then
the outer-man would be at least partially responsible
for knowledge of the material world. Augustine is
clear in maintaining that such is not the case. Sensation is not knowledge. So, the inner-man confronts a
confused amalgam of sensation. How can the inner-man
make sense of these sensations?

We might begin by considering the nature of the
experience that the inner-man confronts. It is always
a difficult task to think in this way, for we have been
structuring experiences into representations of a physical environment all our lives. The environment lends
itself to a coherent and consistent structuring; it can
be made sense of. The environment includes physical
objects and the reports that others make about physical
objects. Such objects are unique. "...it is a characteristic of corporeal substances alone to be condensed and rarefied, contracted and expanded, divided
into small bits and enlarged into a great mass."[43] It
is important for a human being that he know of his

environment because human beings have bodies, and these
bodies are a part of this environment. What, then, must
the inner-man be able to do in order to guarantee the
continued safe existence of the outer-man? This question can be seen as representing a set of related questions.

(1)   What is the overall goal for the outer-man?

(1A) What are the dangers to the outer-man?   (What
      should the inner-man have the outer-man avoid?)

(1B) What are the pleasures of the outer-man?   (What
      should the inner-man have the outer-man pursue?)

(2)   What is the environment of the outer-man?   (What
      are the properties of the world of the outer-man?)

(3)   What role should the testimony of others play in
      knowledge of the material world?

(1) *What is the overall goal that the inner-man ought
to have for the outer-man?*

There are two responses that may be given to this
question. First, the goal is to guarantee the body's
survival in its physical environment. Second, the goal
is to interact with the environment in such a way as to
keep that environment in its proper perspective. These
goals can be seen as leading to two further questions.

(1A) *What are the dangers to the outer-man?   (What
should the inner-man have the outer-man avoid?)*

Consistent with the response to (1), there are two
sources of danger for the outer-man. There are physical dangers, elements in the environment that threaten
the physical safety of the outer-man. There are also
the dangers annexed to the seductive elements of the
physical environment. A too passionate attention to
the objects of sensation distracts the human mind from
eternal truths.

(1B) *Determining the pleasures that the outer-man ought
to pursue* requires an appeal to the metaphysical

elements of Augustine's epistemology. The process of
illumination provides us with eternal ideas. These
ideas are the templates for created things. Human
minds have a deficiency in dealing with concepts; we
are better able to understand the material world than
we are the conceptual world. Thus, we come to understand concepts by understanding the created things for
which they are templates. The outer-man, then, ought
to confront the created world as a basis for knowledge
of eternal ideas. Secondarily, knowledge of the corporeal world is important for its own sake. The inner-
man must be made aware of the immediate environment of
the outer-man for pleasures other than those of *a
priori* knowledge. Augustine writes of the pleasures of
friendship, of his love for Adeodatus, of his regard
for scholarship. All of these require an accurate rendering of the physical world. One sees the inner-man
moderating the intensity of the outer-man's interaction
with the physical world.

(2) *What is the environment of the outer-man? (What
are the properties of the world of the outer-man?)*

The outer-man lives in a world of some regularities and some irregularities. Those regularities that
he encounters are a consequence of the physical world's
being created by God in a manner which is consistent
with His principal ideas. It is not necessary that we
give a theistic analysis of this point. We are considering the role that spiritual vision plays in our
understanding of bodily sensation. The role that it
plays is to provide order and structure to those sensations. This it does by imposing regularities on the
messages sent by the body. Of course, this will be
recognized by those familiar with Idealist attempts to
provide a coherence picture of truth, for Augustine is

offering a coherence model of perception. The images
that are formed in my mind when I see the world are accepted or rejected through appeal to independent standards of judgment -- the divine ideas.

> ...the images of corporeal things...
> which we draw in through the bodily
> sense and which flow in some way into
> memory, and from which things that
> have not been seen are also presented
> to the mind under a fancied image,
> whether it contradicts the reality or
> by chance agrees with it, are approved
> or disapproved within ourselves by
> rules that are wholly different, which
> remain unchangeably above our mind
> when we rightly approve or disapprove
> of anything.[44]

It may be seen that Augustine's account will be prone
to the same difficulties that the Idealists faced:
there are many different templates that may be provided
by the mind to order experience. Which do we choose?
(The criticism of a coherence account of truth that is
usually thought to be fatal amounts to the claim that
there are many different coherent and consistent sets
of propositions that may serve as the standard against
which putatively   e propositions are to be judged.)
We have considere . two aspects of Augustine's account
of perception which bear upon this question. Augustine
thinks perception is useful, and Augustine thinks that
the body's messages provide cues to the spiritual vision for the generation of images. The consistent set
of beliefs that structure previous experiences and mold
future experiences results from this utility and the
physical element in experience. So, there is a

continuous test for the hypothesis about the world that
is formed by the spiritual vision. This test is, basi-
cally, one of utility.

Thus, Augustine is able to consider the random
elements of experience, structure them, and construct a
picture of the physical world, because the goal for
spiritual vision is comprehension. To put the point
directly, in this non-theistic version of Augustine's
account, the world doesn't have to make sense. What
must make sense is our understanding of the world, the
structuring that is accomplished by the spiritual vision.

We have the inner-man imposing a structure on the
manifold of experience, testing that structure, and
modifying it. The resultant structure is reinforced by
two further phenomena. The first involves the unified
nature of sense reports.

Augustine recognizes the unification of the reports of the five different senses. Even though they
are different, "...what one of them informs us also applies to the rest..."[45] Recognizing the unification of
the senses allows Augustine to explain all of the
senses by concentrating on one of them. What does it
mean to say that the senses are unified? One way to
see this point is to maintain that things that look
hard also feel hard, and so on. This begs the question, however, since the test for whether something
looks hard requires recognizing that something feels
hard (one is able to recognize things that feel hard
first, and then one knows what it is to look hard).
An example that comes closest to Augustine's idea of
the unification of the senses would be situations in
which the senses are inter-substitutable. For example, a blind person can substitute touch and hearing

for sight. Someone who is congenitally blind, then, is
clearly not thinking "This feels the way such-and-such
looks (as a sighted person might while navigating in a
darkened room). Touch and hearing, for certain sorts
of information, provide data that would be provided by
sight. This is the sense in which the five senses are
unified.

Augustine expands on this view in *De Libero
Arbitrio*.

> And what of the shapes of bodies? Do
> we not perceive that they are large,
> small, square, round and so on, both
> by touch and sight? Consequently,
> these qualities are not proper either
> to sight or touch alone, but belong to
> both.[46]

So, in providing a unified picture of the world, the
various senses report the same facts about that world.
The unification of the reports of these senses is accomplished by the inner-man's employment of reason. It
also reinforces the structure that the inner-man im-
poses. There is another source of reinforcement.

I have been considering Augustine's epistemology
as an attempt to make sense of a certain kind of input
-- the testimony of the senses. There is another broad
category of input that Augustine considers as well. We
base much of our knowledge of the world on the testimony of others. Thus, we consider our third question.
(3) *What role should the testimony of others play in
my knowledge of the physical world?*

Augustine recognizes that such testimony is essential. "...not only the sense of our own bodies, but
also those of other persons have added very much to our
knowledge."[47] From others we learn such things as

facts about the physical world that we have not experienced (that there is an ocean, information about other cities and peoples), facts about times when we were not alive (historical facts, facts about our birth), and facts about occurrences in familiar parts of the world when we are absent. The testimony of others is essential because it serves to support the view that the world reflects God's divine ideas (on the theistic interpretation) or, it may be seen as further data for the coherent and consistent nature of our understanding of experience (on the non-theistic interpretation). "...we would not know the news that is daily brought to us from everywhere, and is confirmed by evidence that is coherent and convincing..."[48] if we did not avail ourselves of the testimony of others.

This is my analysis of the slogan "The inner-man presides over the body by means of vital attention." What has emerged in responding to these questions is a picture of Augustine's theory of perception as a pragmatic dialectic. A pragmatic dialectic incorporates instruments providing a technique for structuring raw data into a form that is appropriate to a cognitive system with a method for testing and modifying the resultant structure. A pragmatic dialectic is governed by the goals and context of the particular cognitive state. An example might be helpful.

The legal system of the United States incorporates a pragmatic dialectic. One element in that dialectic incorporates a particular goal: We want our laws to be a consequence of inquiry and debate. Thus, we have the technique of legislative reflection and action. This technique is an element in the dialectic that achieves a particular goal. We have another goal: At some point we wish for the laws passed to be utilized;

we do not want an infinite series of inquiries, debates and votes. Thus, we have another instrument within this dialectic: The Supreme Court. It is here that the final inquiry and debate occurs, for there is no appeal beyond action of the Supreme Court. Thus, the goals and context of the legal system of the United States determine the nature of the elements in a pragmatic dialectic.

Augustine's pragmatic dialectic incorporates instruments providing a technique for structuring undifferentiated experience and methods for testing and modifying the resultant structure. This dialectic is identified by the rubric "vital attention." The relationship between the body and the inner-man is a rational one. Contrary to the received view, having the body play a role in the production of mental images does not undermine Augustine's ontology. On the contrary, Augustine's ontological hierarchy is preserved *because* the inner-man is superior to the body, since this superiority guarantees that the inner-man must be aware of all bodily changes. We call the correct operation of the inner-man's vital attention "sensation."

If we bear in mind that *visio spiritualis* is a creative power, we need not feel uncomfortable about the relationship between bodily sight and animal sight. *Visio spiritualis* is both active and passive, in the same way that a landscape painter is both active and passive. Passively, the animal sight receives reports of what goes on in bodily sight, just as a landscape painter passively views a landscape. Actively, spiritual vision generates an image of the object of bodily sight, just as the landscape artist generates a painting actively. In the simplest terms, the inner-man would not be vitalizing the body properly if it were not aware of the changes in the environment of the body.[49]

V

Once an image of a present corporeal object is formed by the spiritual vision the inner-man judges that object by appeal to the eternal truths that are provided by illumination.[50] Non-material, eternal, extra-mental objects permit us to judge material, temporal, extra-mental objects.[51] We shall consider our access to these objects in the next chapter.

Explanation and the Inner-Man

It is at this point that the complexity of Augustine's *visio spiritualis* becomes apparent. This complexity is guaranteed by the attempt to map the dualistic inner/outer dichotomy onto the trinity of visions. There have been several straightforward attempts to accomplish this mapping simply. Unfortunately, they are misleading.

One simplifying solution holds that bodily sight is outer, and there are two inner-visions: spiritual vision, which is the source of our knowledge of material states of affairs, and intellectual vision, which is the source of our knowledge of eternal truths.

Another simplifying solution suggests that bodily sight and animal vision are outer, while intellectual vision is the only inner vision.

Both ideas are plausible only if we suppose that Augustine had a clear concept of the inner/outer distinction, and that he was able to classify all human characteristics as either inner or outer. Further, these accounts depend upon supposing that every human characteristic *is* either exclusively inner or exclusively outer, and that no human aspect can be both. These accounts cannot present an accurate picture of

visio spiritualis because they take it to be
descriptive. In Chapter 2 I argued that the inner/
outer dichotomy is explanatory. The analysis we have
just considered of Augustine's account of perception
reinforces that view. When Augustine is concerned to
explain a human being as a natural phenomenon, as another animal, he takes *visio spiritualis* to be outer.
This permits him to explain our access to material objects as well as the similarity between our transactions with the physical world and the ways in which
animals and the physical world interact. Animal sight
generates images which are representations of the messages delivered by the bodily senses. In this sense
visio spiritualis is taken to be that function of the
human organism which provides access to the material
world.

When Augustine explains how we come to understand
the corporeal world he again writes of *visio spiritualis*, but in these contexts he treats it as the inner
faculty of spiritual vision. He treats spiritual vision as inner because, as the source of images of material states of affairs, it must play a central role in
our judgments of the material world. Our judgments of
the material world, however, go beyond knowing that
certain things are harmful and that certain things are
conducive to life. Animals are also capable of such
judgments, but men are able to understand; they can
know *why* certain things are harmful and other things
are conducive to life. Since it is man's inner faculty that renders such judgments, Augustine uses inner-
man locutions to talk about such judgments. This is
the rationale for writing of *visio spiritualis* as
though it were inner.

Augustine's conception of *visio spiritualis* is
one of his most complicated. *Visio spiritualis* is the

medium that provides us with knowledge of the material
world. It serves in this capacity by receiving messages from the body's senses and by generating images
which are apprehended by the intellectual vision. When
visio spiritualis is serving as the audience for the
bodily senses it is an outer faculty, animal sight.
When it is serving as a generator of images for the intellectual vision it is an inner faculty, spiritual
vision.

In the dual functioning of *visio spiritualis* we
can see most clearly Augustine's notion of a human
being as a unity of the immaterial, spiritual realm and
of the corporeal, temporal realm. On one hand, humans
are taken as natural phenomena, much as beasts and
other created things are natural. As natural phenomena,
humans share certain abilities and traits with the
other animals. One of these abilities allows us to
navigate in a material world. Bodily sight and animal
sight are faculties of our non-human, animal nature.[52]

Augustine's account of sensation can best be
understood within the context of this inner/outer dichotomy and the doctrine of vital attention. In this
context the inner-man locutions work well as a means of
explanation. The central difficulty arises in the context of the generation of images in *visio spiritualis*.
Vital attention provides us with a means of understanding why and how the images are generated. Prin-
cipally, vital attention actively generates images
from the chaos of the messages of sensation in a manner which is consistent with a particular goal. This
aspect of Augustine's treatment of knowledge is not
restricted to sense knowledge and it can be understood
by considering several central distinctions that he
draws.

Augustine's account of knowledge is contrary to
the received contemporary empiricist view. Such a view
reserves "knowledge" for claims that are believed by
someone with good justification when, for all that is
known, the claims are true. On the other hand, basic
knowledge for *Augustine* is belief. Belief is basic because it is temporally prior to understanding.
"...with regard to knowledge...we are necessarily
guided in a two-fold way, by authority and by reason.
Temporally, authority is first..."[53]   Augustine is
pointing out that we do not seek knowledge in a vacuum.
We begin with beliefs that we hope to support; belief
for Augustine requires the active acceptance of an
authority.[54]

Augustine draws the distinction between knowledge
and ignorance in terms of the difference between seeing
a thing and not seeing a thing;[55]   as a failure to
achieve rather than as the absence of some thing. This
is consistent with Augustine's view that the objects of
knowledge are always present and that the responsibility for ignorance lies solely with the mind. Coming to
know, then, is an active process. This view can perhaps best be seen by contrasting it with an alternative, an acquisition approach to knowledge. Such an
approach maintains that some *thing* (thought, mental
image, concept) which was absent in ignorance or truth
is always present to the inner-man, so that ignorance
is not explained as lack of access but as lack of dis-
cernment.

When one comes to know it is through the application of reason. Reason, for Augustine, is taken in
several ways.

Reason is the sight of the mind by
means of which the mind is able to

> apprehend truth, by itself and without
> help from the body; or, reason is the
> contemplating itself of truth, without
> the help of the body; or reason is
> truth itself which is apprehended.[56]

The distinction between reason and knowledge is given
in terms of the distinction between looking and seeing.
"...looking is one thing, seeing another...Applying
this distinction to the mind, we call one thing reason,
the other knowledge..."[57] Reason is an activity of the
soul which is successful when one comes to know. One
comes to know when reason has rendered clear what pre-
viously had been confused.

What, then, occurs when vital attention operates?
Visio corporis presents confusedly a sensation to the
inner-man. Using cues (in particular, those cues associated with the preservation of the life of the
outer-man) the inner-man constructs an image representing a likely, coherent, systematic picture of the
physical world. The physical world was constructed by
God in accord with His divine ideas. Thus, the physical world is formally harmonious -- it makes sense. In
order to represent this world accurately, the inner-man
must construct a picture of the world that itself is
harmonious. With this picture the inner-man is able to
adequately navigate the body through its environment.

In light of this account of Augustine's treatment
of knowledge of the material world, his kinship to
later philosophers is interesting to consider. We
might see him as a non-Solipsistic Leibniz or a worldly
Kant. In fact, taking this portion of his epistemology
in conjunction with his treatment of memory and of *a
priori* knowledge, one profitable way to think of him
is to see him offering a pragmatically grounded

Idealism. That is, one can see Augustine as treating
our knowledge of the material world as being a consequence of our representing the world by means of ideas
that work.

Chapter 5

Footnotes

[1] DQA 25, 49; 30, 58.

[2] See, for example, the long discussion beginning at CO X, 30; EP 18; DVR 10, 18.

[3] ...*habens de rebus quas mente atque ratione comprehendit, etiamsi parvam propter corpus corruptibile, quod adgravat animam (quoniam, sicut apostolus, ex parte scimus), tamen certissimam scientiam creditque sensibus in rei cuiusque evidentia quibus per corpus animus utitur, quoniam miserabilius fallitur qui numquam putat eis credendum...* DCD XIX, 18; See also DT XV, 12, 21.

[4] *Vivacitas sentiendi est, qua magis alius, alius minus in ipsis corporalibus rebus pro earum modo atque natura quod verum est percipit, atque id a falso magis minusue discernit. Contra Julianum* IV, 14, 65.

[5] DT XI, 8, 13.

[6] DT XV, 12, 21.

[7] ...*in quibus tam multa aliter sunt quam videntur...* DT XV, 12, 21.

[8] See, for example, Armstrong, A.H., (ed.) *Later Greek and Early Medieval Philosophy*. Cambridge University Press, 1970, p. 376; Nash, R.H., *The Light of the Mind*. The University Press of Kentucky, 1969, Ch. 4; Gannon, M.A.I., "The Active Theory of Sensation in St. Augustine," *The New Scholasticism* (April 1956).

[9] *Mirare potius quod facere aliquid in anima corpus potest. De Musica* (hereafter DMU) VI, 4, 7.

[10] *Illud me conturbat, quomodo sonantes numeri, qui certe corporei sunt, vel quoquo modo in corpore, magis,*

*laudandi sint quam illi, qui, cum sentimus, in anima
esse reperiuntur.* DMU VI, 4, 7.

[11] DIA 16, 25; DQA 33, 70.

[12] DT IX, 6, 10-7, 12.

[13] *Cum igitur tria sint rerum genera quae videntur;
unum corporalium...alterum simile corporalibus...tertium
ab utroque discretum, quod neque...ullam habeat
similitudinem corporis...* EP 120, 2, 11.

[14] *...quique notissimis nuntiis corporis...* DUC I,
1.

[15] *...pertinet corporis sensus ad visa corporalia...*
DGAL XII, 16, 32.

[16] DGAL XII, 24.

[17] DT XI, 2, 3.

[18] *...omnes corporis sensus cordi intro nuntient
quid senserint foris...* IJE XVIII, 10.

[19] *...aliud esse aspectum aliud visionem...* DQA 27,
53.

[20] *Sensu enim nos bestiae multae superant, cujus rei
causam non hic locus est ut quaeramus; mente autem,
ratione, scientia, nos illis Deus praeposuit. Sed ille
sensus ea quibus tales animae delectantur, accedente
consuetudine cujus magna vis est, potest discernere;
atque eo facilius, quod anima belluarum magis corpori
affixa est, cujus illi sunt sensus quibus utitur ad
victum voluptatemque, quam ex eodem illo corpore capit.*
DQA 28, 54.

[21] *...ut et signa rerum formarentur in spiritu, et
eorum refulgeret intellectus in mente; secundum hanc,
inquam, distinctionem spirituable nunc appellavimus
tale genus visorum, quali etiam corporum absentium
imagines cogitamus.* DGAL XII, 9, 20.

[22]
...*sicut cogitatio formare potuerit.*   DGAL XII,
6, 15.

[23]
   Aliter enim cogitamus Carthaginem quam novimus,
aliter Alexandriam quam non novimus.   DGAL XII, 6, 15.

[24]
...*ex illo uno modo quem invenimus in Epistola and*
Corinthios, quo spiritus a mente ditinguitur evidentis-
simo testimonio.   Si enim oravero, inquir, lingua,
apiritus meus orat, mens autem mea infructuosa est.
DGAL XII, 8, 19.

[25]
...*obscuras et mysticas significationes, a quibus*
si intellectum mentis removeas, nemo aedificatur,
audiendo quod non intellegit...   DGAL XII, 8, 19.

[26]
   A specie quippe corporis quod cernitur, exoritur
ea quae fit in sunsu cernentis; et ab hac, ea quae fit
in memoria; et ab hac, ea quae fit in acie cogitantis.
DT XI, 9, 16.

[27]
   DT XI, 2, 3.

[28]
   DGAL XII, 20.

[29]
...*sensus non procedat ex corpore illo quod*
videntur, sed ex corpore sentientis animantis, cui
anima suo quodam miro modo contemperatur...sed etiam
sensus informatus sit, quae visio vocatur.   DT XI, 2, 3.

[30]
   DMU VI, 6, 16.

[31]
...*praesides judicent...*   EP 147, 41.

[32]
...*quadam vitali intentione...*   EP 122, 2.

[33]
   DGAL III, 16, 25.

[34]
   DMU VI, 5, 9-10; DQA 33, 71; DGAL VII, 19, 25.

[35]
...*tamen ex corpore quod videtur giguitur visio...*
DT XI, 2, 3.

[36]
*...sensus ipse formatur; ut jam non tantum sensus
...sed etiam sensus informatus sit, quae visio vocatur.*
DT XI, 2, 3.

[37]
*...ex visibili et vidente gignitur visio, ita sane
ut ex vidente sit sensus oculorum, et aspicientis atque
intuentis intentio: illa tamen informatio sensus, quae
visio dicitur... DT XI, 2, 3.*

[38]
*Ideoque non possumus quidem dicere quod sensum
gignat res visibilis: giguit tamen formam velut
similitudinem suam, quae fit in sensu, cum aliquid
videndo sentimus. DT XI, 2, 3.*

[39]
*...ut in corpore fiat, et per corpus in anima;
fit enim in sensu, qui neque sine corpore est, neque
sine anima. DT XI, 2, 5.*

[40]
*...neque enim omnino inde gignitur, quoniam
aliquid aliud adhibetur corpori, ut ex illo formetur,
id est sensus videntis. DT XI, 5, 9.*

[41]
*...pro illa specie corporis...succedit memoria
retinens illam speciem quam per corporis sensum
combibit anima; proque illa visione quae foris erat cum
sensus ex corpore sensibili formaretur, succedit intus
similis visio, cum ex eo quod memoria tenet... DT XI,
3, 6.*

[42]
...haec omnis silva... SO II, 6, 11.

[43]
*Ac per hoc densari ac rarescere, contrahi et
dilatari, in minutias deteri et grandescene in molem,
non nisi corporum est. EP 137, II, 4.*

[44]
*...phantasias rerum corporalium per corporis
sensum haustas, et quodam modo infusas memoriae, ex
quibus etiam ea quae non visa sunt, ficto phantasmate
cogitantur, sive aliter quam sunt, sive fortuitu sicuti
sunt, aliis omnino regulis supra mentem nostram*

incummutabiliter manentibus, vel approbare apud nosme
tipsos, vel improbare aliquid approbamus aut improbamus.
DT IX, 6, 10.

45
    Quod enim nobis unus eorum renuntiat, etiam in
eaeteris valet. DT XI, 1, 1.

46
    Quid corporum formas, magnas, breves, quadras,
rotundas, et si quid hujusmodi est, nonne et tangendo et
videndo sentimus, et ideo nec taetui tribui possunt,
sed utrique? DLA II, 3, 8.

47
    ...non solum nostrorum, verum etiam et alienorum
corporum sensus plurimum addidisse nostrae scientiae
confitendum est. DT XV, 12, 21.

48
    ...nescimus quae quotidie undecumque nuntiantur,
et indiciis consonis contestantibusque firmantur...
DT XV, 12, 21.

49
Discussions supporting this view may be found at
DVR 41, 77; DGAL VII, 25, 36; EP 166, 2.

50
  DCD XI, 27, 2.

51
  DT XII, 2, 2; EP 166.

52
  See, for example, DQA 27, 53.

53
    Sequitur ut dicam quomodo studiosi erudiri
debeant, qui sicut dictum est vivere instituerunt. Ad
discendum item necessario dupliciter ducimur,
auctoritate atque ratione. Tempore auctoritas, re
autem ratio prior est. DO II, 9, 26.

54
    De Spiritu et Littera XXXI, 54.

55
  DQA 27, 53.

56
    Ratio est aspectus animi, quo per seipsum, non
per corpus verum intuetur; aut ipsa veri contemplatio,
non per corpus; aut ipsum verum quod contemplatur.
DIA VI, 10. See also, SE 43, 2.

[57]
...*aliud esse aspectum, aliud visionem; quae duo in mente rationem et scientiam nominamus.* DQA 30, 58.

CHAPTER 6

ILLUMINATION
A *Priori* Knowledge and Order

Many knowledge claims deal neither with the past nor with the physical environment. These knowledge claims seem to owe their truth to something other than contingent states of affairs -- they have been thought to be necessary in some sense, and to be independent of experience. No matter what the characteristics of the physical world are, and no matter what has occurred in the past, these necessarily true propositions have always been, are, and will continue to be true. Necessary truths are important because they apply to the non-necessary, contingent aspect of human experience. Augustine accounts for our access to necessary truths with his theory of illumination.

                                   I

At the outset, it is important to note a contemporary controversy concerning the existence of necessary truths. Some philosophers -- most notably, Willard van Orman Quine -- have maintained that the necessary truth/contingent truth distinction is a false distinction. It is a false distinction because there are no necessary truths. That the sentence "This book is identical with itself" is true is a consequence of a fact about this universe: Things are identical with themselves. The universe might be some

other way -- it might be the case that the universe is
so constituted that things are *not* identical with themselves. Thus, self-identity is a contingent fact about
the universe, as is any principle that serves as the
basis for an allegedly necessary truth. Thus, the necessary truth/contingent truth distinction is a spurious
one.

In light of this position, it might be argued that
the distinction drawn by Augustine is not worth considering, since it is a distinction that we -- in our
enlightened condition -- no longer draw. There are two
reasons for rejecting this suggestion. First, the position that there are no necessary truths continues to
be a minority position among philosophers. There are
those who maintain, in fact, that there could not be a
universe for which the principle of identity, the law
of excluded middle, and the principle of non-contradic-
tion do not hold. Second, a genuine distinction of
some sort is, in fact, being drawn, even though it may
not be the necessary/contingent distinction. There are
some beliefs that I hold that are independent of experience. For example, my belief that the sum of two
million and two million is four million is a belief I
hold firmly, even though I have never (consciously) experienced two million things. I shall continue to believe that one and one are two, even though I might see
one cloud join another cloud to form one cloud. There
are some beliefs that are independent of experience
both for their establishment and for their continued
application, to which, nonetheless, we hold experience
answerable. If we deny that these beliefs are necessarily true, we must be prepared to account for their
truth in some other way.

More importantly, for Augustine, these truths
form the bases for unique kinds of judgment that are

not arrived at in the same way that judgments of
contingent states of affairs are. If I say to you
"There are at least three charmed Quarks in this room"
the truth or falsity of that sentence will be determined by a fact about the room. There may not be any
charmed Quarks at all, in which case the sentence will
be false. There may be one or two charmed Quarks in
this room, in which case the sentence will be false.
There may be three or billions of charmed Quarks in
this room -- and the sentence would be true. The basis
for these judgments are operations of a certain sort:
determining whether a particular theory is correct;
counting the number of a certain sort of object. Suppose that I say, "There are at least three charmed
Quarks in this room or there are not at least three
charmed Quarks in this room." We can all agree that
this sentence is true.

All this amounts to is saying that whether or not
the necessary/contingent distinction is a genuine one
(and I must add at this point that I find arguments
maintaining that it is not unconvincing) it is a useful
distinction about modes of judging. Augustine's discussion of principal ideas and illumination is a discussion of standards of judgment and our access to
these standards. In this chapter I will consider his
account of our access to the standards of judgment --
his theory of illumination. In the next chapter I will
consider Augustine's account of judgment.

II

After presenting Augustine's theory of illumination as he presented it, I shall turn to an interpretation of that theory that I feel renders it consistent
with Augustine's position as I have sketched it thus
far. I am not concerned to provide a detailed account

of alternative interpretations of Augustine on
illumination, although I will mention what the alternative positions are. I do not consider alternative positions for three reasons. First, this has been done
very well by others (I have footnoted the better di-
gests of the respective positions). Second, it seems
to me that literature on illumination has grown like
Topsy, so that we have Ronald Nash's view of Gilson's
view of Aquinas' view of Augustine on illumination.
All of these views are instructive, and I commend them
to the reader. However, the snowball has to stop some-
where, and I have decided that I don't want to add to
this controversy. Finally, my position on illumination
is a segment of my broader picture of Augustine's epistemology. It seems fruitless to compare my view with
the views of all these others, since their treatments
of illumination have not been advanced in the same context.

        With this in mind, let me indicate something about
previous positions on illumination.

        There has been controversy in the literature (both
historical and recent) concerning what it is that
illumination accomplishes -- over what it is that
illumination provides us. Some (the ontologists) have
maintained that God is directly responsible for the
principal ideas occurring in the individual human mind.
Others (the concordantists) have held that the result
of illumination is indirect -- God creating objects
and human minds abstracting principal ideas from these
objects. More recently, scholars (the formalists)
have held that illumination does not give man principal ideas either directly or indirectly. Rather,
illumination applies to the epistemic status of some
of our judgments -- whether they are certain or necessary.[1]

Among all of the discussions of illumination I
have encountered, Professor Ronald Nash's comes closest
to the one I shall advance. Professor Nash recognizes
an active element in man's knowledge of principal
ideas. The problem with his interpretation is that it
doesn't recognize the *significant* activity involved in
such knowledge. The activity that he writes of is the
activity involved in judging the material object by
appeal to the form. "Thus for Augustine, human knowledge of sensible things is more than mere sensation.
It is an active relating of the thing sensed to eternal
standards, the forms."[2]

We have seen that Augustine's theory of perception
includes a significant and interesting active element.
His account of our knowledge of principal ideas includes an active element also, but it is not the one
that Professor Nash mentions.

In his commentary on the Gospel of John, *In
Johannis Evangelium*, Augustine, observing that, "One
man in the East understands justice, another man in the
West understands justice..."[3] wonders whether "...the
justice one man understands is a different thing from
that which the other understands."[4] In *De Libero
Arbitrio* Augustine asks Evodius whether "...something
can be found which is seen in common by all who reason,
each with his own reason and mind..."[5] which has the
properties of being "...present to all and is not
changed for the use of those to whom it is present..."[6]
and which "...remains uncorrupted and whole whether
they see it or do not see it..."[7] What puzzles
Augustine is that several individuals may know facts
which have a peculiar property -- knowing them is independent of experience and such knowledge seems certain. When we know about material objects we may

point to the objects of such knowledge. Augustine
wonders whether there might not be objects for *a priori*
knowledge as well.

His answer is that we have access to special objects which we do not experience *via* the body's senses.
In the case of men who have a notion of justice, "In
body they are far apart, and yet they have the eyes of
their minds on one object..."[8] Men are able to know
such things because

> ...we have another and far higher
> perception which is interior, and
> by which we distinguish what is
> just from what is unjust, what is
> just by means of an intellectual
> conception, what is unjust by lack
> of such a form.[9]

Evodius' answer to Augustine's question is that mathematical truths are examples of such truths. We have
seen that in addition the certainty that one is alive
is a truth which no experience can undermine. "...{I}t
is clear to you that you are..."[10] These truths, or
principal ideas, are those mysterious objects which are
neither material objects nor images of material objects.

In condensed form Augustine presents his analysis
of *Ideae Principales* (principal ideas, *species*, reasons, *formae*) in question 46 of *De diversis Quaestionibus LXXXIII, De Ideis*. This is the key passage:
"...the principal ideas are certain images, or stable
and unchangeable reasons of things, which not being
themselves formed are consequently eternal and always
the same, and are contained in the Divine Intelligence."[11] Augustine suggests that these ideas have
several important properties. They are eternal. They

are immutable. They are the source of change, becoming, and ending. They are located in the Divine Intelligence. The passage in *De Ideis* that argues for these various properties is one of his more subtle discussions. Augustine argues that God has fashioned all things rationally and that some things change. From the former it follows that all change is ordered, controlled, and governed by His laws. Thus, nothing happens which is not founded on His laws. From the latter proposition, and from the assumption that things neither come into existence from nothing, nor go out of existence to nothing, Augustine holds that everything that begins and ends does so, eventually, from things that have no beginning and no end. If nothing outside of the mind of God creates, and if all change in created things is founded in principal ideas, then the eternal ideas that govern the universe must be His ideas. They must be ideas that are had by the mind of God.

There is a Platonic element in this account. Principal ideas serve as templates in the generation of material objects. "We behold then, by the sight of the mind, in that eternal truth from which all things temporal are made, the form according to which we exist, and according to which we do anything by true and right reason..."[12] When he goes on to give his account of *how* all things temporal are made, he appeals to a notion of "participation" in eternal ideas.

Having asserted that there are principal ideas and that we have access to such ideas, Augustine then asks whether "...truth itself, which the mind confronts without the use of the body, exists by itself and is not in the mind, or whether it can exist without the mind."[13] He wonders whether truth is located

in something like a Platonic heaven or whether it is in
fact possible for an idea of any sort to exist without
a mind's "having" it.

> If it were in this place where our
> body is, a man in the East who makes
> judgments about bodies in the same
> way (we do) would not see it. There-
> fore, it is not thus contained in
> space. It is everywhere present to
> one who judges. It is no place, and
> it is no place absent in potentiality.[14]

In *De Trinitate* he suggests that

> ...they abide not as if fixed in one
> place, as are bodies, but as intel-
> ligible things in incorporeal nature.
> They are so at hand to the glance of
> the mind, as things visible or tan-
> gible in place are to the sense of
> the body.[15]

So, truth, wherever it is, is not located spatially,
"...nor does it play through time, nor wander to
places, nor is it interrupted by night, nor shut off by
shadows, nor is it subject to the senses of the body."[16]
When Augustine wishes to provide a positive characterization of principal ideas or truth he tells us that

> ...it is very near to all, to all
> everlasting. It is in no place. It
> is never away. It admonishes openly.
> It teaches inwardly. It changes all
> who see it to the better. By none
> is it changed to the worse. No one
> judges of it. Without it no one
> judges well.[17]

In Augustine's analysis of these peculiar ideas,
his account of their characteristics and his

explanation of our access to them, the inner-man
locutions once again play a centrally important role.
Augustine holds that "Truth dwells in the inner-man."[18]
"Those things that are comprehended by the intellect
are comprehended as existing nowhere else but in the
comprehending mind itself and, at the same time, as not
contained in space."[19]   Locating principal ideas in the
mind allows Augustine to explain our access to them by
using inner-man locutions. "The soul can only contem-
plate them with its higher part, that is to say, its
mind and reason, and as it were with a certain vision
or interior intellectual eye."[20]   These ideas are objects of inner-vision for two reasons. We have already
considered the first: the principal ideas serve as
standards of judgment when we judge the physical world.
"...it is by this latter power {illumination} that objects of a lower order are judged..."[21]   Principal
ideas are the proper objects of inner-vision for another reason.

> ...the gift of this vision to the
> intellectual soul is not to enable
> it to see anything and everything
> it wishes, but what is holy and
> pure. The soul has this eye by
> which are seen healthy, genuine,
> and calm things...[22]

Augustine maintains the view that principal ideas are
the proper objects of inner-vision because he holds
that "...reason is the sight of the mind..."[23]   "by
means of which it beholds truth, by itself and without
help of the body."[24]   (Reason can also be "...the contemplation itself of the true, without aid of the
body, and the true itself, which it beholds.")[25]

So, principal ideas allow us to judge the material world. They are also worth studying for their

own sake. What emerges at this point, once again, is
Augustine's concern for order and structure in knowledge. The universe has been created by God consistent
with the perfect divine ideas (we saw in the previous
chapter that a non-theistic version of this point can
be made). Thus, the universe is ordered. The problem
for human knowledge becomes one of gaining access to
this order, and, since the principal ideas are the
source of this order, we can gain access to the order
by attending to principal ideas.

III

     In our earlier consideration of the senses of the
inner-man we noted that Augustine discusses inner-sight
and inner-hearing almost exclusively. It is in the
context of his discussion of principal ideas that we
find the rationale for excluding other inner senses.
"...{W}hat is grasped with the intellect is within the
mind, and having it is equivalent to seeing."[26]   Why
does Augustine wish to maintain this? Principal ideas
are objects of eternal truth which correspond in important ways to the objects of corporeal knowledge. There
are also some disanalogies. These objects are eternal,
unchanging, non-spatial. Augustine explains our access
to such objects by using inner-man locutions, but he
must choose his explanations with care, because he is
trying to explain access to objects that have unique
properties. He preserves these properties and explains
our access to these ideas by speaking of inner-sight
and inner-hearing.

> Less like the truth, therefore, are
> all those things that we touch or
> taste or smell, and more like it
> those things that we see or hear;
> because every word is heard whole

> by all those by whom it is heard,
> and heard whole by each at the
> same time, and every visible ob-
> ject that is before the eyes is
> seen at the same time, as much by
> one as by another.[27]

A priori knowledge takes objects. Many people must be
able to have access to these objects, and the objects
must be unchanged when they become known by individual
minds. In perception the objects of sight and hearing
may be shared, and seeing and hearing these objects
does not change them. The objects of the other bodily
senses do not have these two properties. The objects
of taste, for example, are available to only one person
at a time. Two people may eat from the same food, but
they may not eat the same bit of food. Two people may
touch the same object, but not in the same place at the
same time. Two people may smell the same scent, but
not from the exact same bit of air. In addition,
smelling and tasting change the objects which are
smelled and tasted.

Augustine's wish that his explanation show how
"...the whole (of truth) is at one time common to all"[28]
raises two problems. One problem is expressible in
contemporary terms. Its solution raises a further
problem that was recognized by Malebranche.[29]

The contemporary problem rests upon the recognition that minds are mutually inaccessible, that my
thoughts are private (in the sense that only I can
have them). If things within the mind are inaccessible
to other minds, then locating principal ideas inwardly
undermines Augustine's desire that they be "at one time
common to all." More unpleasantly for Augustine's
epistemology, even if the things in my mind are the

same as the things in your mind, I could never know
that they are.

It may be objected that this criticism is unfair
to Augustine. After all, Augustine can hardly be held
accountable for not having read Wittgenstein. Unfortunately, Augustine did recognize just this sort of
privacy. He tells us in *De Libero Arbitrio* that
"...neither do I see anything of your mind, nor you
anything of mine..."[30]

Augustine's solution to this difficulty is fairly
straightforward. Since ideas do not exist independently of minds, principal ideas must be had by a mind
in order to exist. But principal ideas are eternal,
immutable, perfect, and our own minds, although eternal,
are changeable. Thus, principal ideas must be had by
an eternal, immutable mind as well as by my mind. As
Augustine tells us, principal ideas "...are contained
in the Divine Intelligence."[31] But Augustine is not
solving the problem of mutual inaccessibility to principal ideas by saying that these ideas are in God's
mind, we all have access to these ideas, so we all have
access to the same objects. This cannot be Augustine's
solution because such a solution leads to unfortunate
problems. First, the reference to truth or eternal
ideas as being within us occur too frequently in
Augustine's work to make such a solution reasonable.
When we come to know it is by means of an interior object. If Augustine thought that knowing eternal truths
involved seeing the mind of God he would have said so.
Augustine could not say that knowing eternal truths involves access to the Divine Mind for a second reason,
expressed by Malebranche. Simply stated, Augustine
could not hold that knowledge of mathematics, for example, involved access to the Divine Mind because
mathematical truths can be used for evil purposes.

In fact, there is good reason to suppose that
Augustine thought that the Divine Ideas are ideogenetic,
creating the ideas in the human mind *via* which mathematical propositions, for example, are known and corporeal things are judged.[32]   One argument that
Augustine gives for God's existence depends upon our
recognizing that we mutable things can know immutable
truths.

> Thus you would certainly not deny
> that there is an immutable truth,
> containing all things which are
> immutably true, which you can not
> say is yours or mine or any one
> else's but presents itself in com-
> mon to all who discern immutable
> truths...[33]

Since we are mutable these truths must have some unchanging source, and this source is God.   Thus,
Augustine is able to maintain the mutual inaccessibility of minds on one hand and the mutual accessibility
of an object of knowledge on the other.

However, "Divine Ideas are ideogenetic" is another
slogan, and, while avoiding two important problems,
brings us full circle to the original problems: How do
we know eternal truths?   How are our principal ideas
generated by God's Divine Ideas?

IV

There are similarities between Augustine's account
of eternal truth and Plato's theory of forms.   However,
Augustine's view diverges from Plato's, perhaps most
importantly, in his account of how the human mind gains
access to principal ideas.   He agrees with Plato that
"...we have a kind of knowledge of certain things
stored up in the recesses of the mind..."[34]   However,

when he turns his attention specifically to the slave
boy in the *Meno* he rejects *anamnesis* as the source of
knowledge of eternal truths by rejecting access to
eternal truths in a previous life. Plato tried to show
us that men's souls lived before men had bodies.
Rather than *learning* eternal truths, we remember eternal truths. But the argument in the *Meno* will not
work, says Augustine. Geometricians are rare in this
life, so there is good reason to suppose that they were
rare in the previous life. The slave boy is supposed
to be recollecting his proof, but in order to recollect
his proof the slave boy must have been a geometrician
in his earlier life. Socrates just made a lucky
choice, for had the slave boy not been a geometrician
in his earlier life he could not have remembered the
proof in this one. Thus, the *Meno* does not establish
recollection as the source of knowledge of eternal
truths.[35]

Why does Augustine so misconstrue Plato's point in
the *Meno*? He may be making a joke, or, he may be
thinking of the Platonic notion that each person has a
specific role to which he is best suited, supposing
that Plato somehow intended for this doctrine to extend
to the realm of the forms. I am inclined to favor the
former explanation, but, whatever his reason for advancing this criticism of *anamnesis*, it is his replace-
ment for it -- illumination -- which concerns us here.

According to Augustine, the mind may be seen as
standing in a special set of relationships to a kind of
incorporeal light. He frequently describes ignorance
as a darkness of the soul which is relieved by a kind
of light. "...{W}hat I know of myself I know through
the shining of your light. And what I do not know of
myself I continue not to know until my darkness is made

like noon time in your presence."[36]   Without access to
this incorporeal light man is ignorant.   "...{O}ur mind,
which is the eye of the soul, unless it is irradiated
by the light of truth...will not be able to come to
wisdom nor to righteousness."[37]   Illumination provides
us with the possibility to know all of those things we
claim to know, whether they are *a priori* truths or our
knowledge of material objects.

> The light itself by which we dis-
> tinguish all this, by which we are
> made aware of what we believe with-
> out knowing it, what we hold as
> objects of knowledge, what physical
> shape we recall, what one we imagine,
> what the sense-organ perceives, what
> the mind imagines in the likeness of
> a body, what is present to the intel-
> lect as certain yet totally unlike
> any physical object, this light by
> which all these mental acts are dif-
> ferentiated...shines invisibly and
> indescribably, yet intelligibly, and
> it is as certain a fact itself as are
> the realities which we see as certain
> by means of it.[38]

This light illumines eternal truths in such a way that
it is possible for all human minds to know them.
"...{T}here are true and immutable rules of numbers,
the reason and truth of which...is immutably present
to all perceivers in common..."[39]   Unfortunately, although "...the sun shines on the face of those who can
see and on the face of those who are blind...both are
not able to see. One sees the other does not see..."[40]
Thus, one view of illumination is that it provides the

opportunity for knowledge, the way that the sun or a
physical light provides the opportunity for knowing
about material objects. The inner-eye sees eternal
truths in much the same way "...that the bodily eye
sees things near to it in bodily light, the light for
which it is made to be receptive..."[41] The comparison
of illumination to a physical light helps us to understand some of the relationships that stand between illumination and knowledge. Some of what we learn about
things is governed by how well we can see them. So,
too, this special light "...shines upon our mind and
enables us to make correct judgments by all other
things. For the ability to judge is proportionate to
our ability to receive this light."[42] But illumination
only makes knowing *possible*; other conditions must be
fulfilled as well. Before we can consider what these
might be we must consider some other things that
Augustine wrote about illumination.

Sometimes Augustine writes of illumination as
though it were truth itself. "Truth itself is the
light of the mind."[43] "...{T}he form itself of un-
shaken and stable truth...sheds in an immoveable eter-
nity...the light of incorruptible and most sound
reason..."[44] "...{H}e that does the truth comes to the
light..."[45]

Sometimes Augustine writes as though wisdom were
the light. "I know that wisdom is an incorporeal substance, and that it is the light by which those things
are seen that are not seen by bodily eyes..."[46]

Thus, the light would seem to be either a condition which is necessary for knowledge of truth, or the
object of such knowledge. Augustine recognizes that
his various discussions of "the light" might be taken
in these two ways and is prepared to explain how it

may be so taken by a further appeal to how physical
lights work.

> The light shows both other things
> and itself also. You light a
> lamp, for example, to look for
> your coat, and the burning lamp
> gives you light to find your coat.
> Do you light the lamp to see it
> when it burns? A burning lamp is
> capable of revealing to view other
> things which were covered by dark-
> ness and of also showing itself to
> your eyes at the same time.[47]

There is not a real distinction between truth and one
necessary condition for knowing truth. It is not that
there is some special source of illumination which
falls upon the objects of inner-vision and thus makes
them available to the inner-eye. Rather, the objects
of inner-vision provide their own illumination. It is
as though each eternal truth were a lamp.

This point may be made in another way. In Chapter
3 we considered the elements in the traditional analysis of knowledge claims. I argued that there was no
need to draw a distinction between a particular fact's
being adequately justified and that fact's being true.
I claimed that the analysis includes a redundancy. In
illumination theory Augustine is saying the same thing.
When an idea has been presented by illumination it
thereby becomes true. Nothing more need be said about
it. So, truth and being illuminated come to the same
thing.

With these observations in mind we can examine
illumination as an explanation of the ideogenetic nature of principal ideas. Our problem is to explain

the relationship between Divine Ideas and the ideas
that human minds perceive without requiring direct access to God's mind. The doctrine of illumination accomplishes this. We may see how illumination does this
by reconsidering how an ordinary physical light comes
to reveal physical objects to an observer. The sun
does not somehow actively implant the perception of
trees in our minds; it only makes it possible for us to
see trees. The sun (or some other source of light) is
a necessary condition for our seeing trees, but it is
not sufficient. Other conditions must be operative as
well: conditions of the environment, conditions of the
observer. The case of illumination and understanding
is simpler but analogous. Principal ideas provide all
of the necessary conditions for their being known except those that pertain to the individual knower.
Principal ideas no more actively implant themselves in
human minds than does the sun actively implant knowledge of trees in the bodily sight. Illumination provides the human mind with all of the pre-conditions for
understanding except those that are provided by the
understanding mind.

Augustine's account of *a priori* knowledge contains
a number of characteristics that are central to his
epistemology. Augustine's theories of memory and perception were both characterized in active terms. This
volitional theme is continued in his analysis of *a
priori* knowledge, for he holds that human beings are
responsible for turning their attention to the eternal
truths that illumination reveals. God provides the
potential for understanding, but the achievement of
understanding is the individual person's. At this
point, however, analogies between the account of perception of the material world and perception of the

world of divine ideas cease. One can make sense of the
view that our knowledge of corporeals does not proceed
directly from the material objects themselves but,
rather, is a consequence of the mind's interacting with
the body and creating an image. However, if it is true
that the relationship of illumination is ideogenetic,
so that the illuminated mind has ideas of its own that
are generated by the principal ideas, then it looks as
though the inner-man is apprehending objects which are
caused by the mind of God. It looks as though
Augustine is advancing a causal view of *a priori* knowledge. In turn, this seems to rule out *a priori* knowledge as being creative.

One approach to Augustine on principal ideas is to
see his account as a treatment of the problem of general terms. When I assert that a particular object is a
member of a class, I apply a general term -- a term
that refers to many things -- to one thing. This is
why the term is general. Augustine gives such assertions meaning as a consequence of an inner comparison.
The inner-man compares the mental image constructed by
the spiritual vision with the idea that has been generated by illumination. This comparison is similar to
the comparison which is central to John Locke's analysis of the meaning of general terms. The problem with
such accounts is that they seem to presuppose an ability to classify in the process of explaining this
ability. Here is how the theory is supposed to work.
If I say "Evodius is a man," my judgment will be correct if my mental image of Evodius agrees with my mental image of being a man. So, once I have formed my
mental image of Evodius and conjure my image of humanity, I compare the two. If as a consequence of this
comparison I see that the images agree, then I am able

to say "Evodius is a man." But how do I arrive at the
correct general idea which I compare my image of
Evodius to? It must be because I am able to classify
from among all of the candidates first, general ideas,
and second, my general idea of humanity. It is easy to
see that this leads to a regress of classification.

This problem for other systems of classification
might be expressed in Augustine's terms as follows.
When I judge, how do I know that I am using the correct
principal idea as my standard of judgment? There is a
theistic way to deal with this problem. Augustine
might respond that we know we are using the correct
principal idea because divine illumination guarantees
it. Appropriate care in the study of that which illumination reveals, where that care is due to religious
faith, will provide the proper principal idea. There
is a non-theistic account that may be given as well.

VI

In his epistemology Augustine uses principal ideas
for two purposes. First, they serve as standards of
judgment for the material world. Second, they provide
information (about mathematical and geometrical truths,
for example) that applies to any world. These ideas,
then, are central to the cognitive system that
Augustine constructs. This system, as we have seen, is
rationally structured. [48] Principal ideas constitute
the key to that structure. The role of principal ideas
in the theistic model was that of a template or blueprint. Principal ideas served as the plan in terms of
which God constructed the world. The non-theistic approach to illumination I propose explains illumination
differently.

The Cartographic Model: A blueprint anticipates
and determines a system by representing that system

graphically. The properties of the system result from
the blueprint. Maps are related to the systems they
represent in the opposite way. In primary mapping
(i.e., mapping virgin territory) the first stage involves surface exploration, surveying and aerial pho-
tography. One begins with a system which is to be
represented graphically as a consequence of primary encounters. Once a provisional map is drafted it is sub-
jected to a comparison with the topography in order to
determine whether that area of the earth is accurately
represented. Discrepancies are resolved by modifica-
tion of the map. (Imagine a mapmaker who, having made
a mistake in his map, bulldozed a hill to make his map
correct!) On the other hand, in blueprinting (although
here, too, the blueprint might be modified under certain circumstances) it is the system that must reflect
the blueprint.

We may consider Augustine's theory of illumination
in terms of this cartographic model. We have seen that
his theory of perception includes a strong pragmatic
element. The structures exhibited by the images in
spiritual vision were due to the requirement that the
soul preserve the integrity of the body. The structuring was governed by principal ideas; the ideas that
illumination reveals provide the foundation for structuring experience both in terms of the physical world
and in terms of facts that are applicable to any world.
How are these ideas formed? One might see the mind as
constructing hypotheses that are candidates for the
maps that will structure experience. (Think, for example, of the famous passage in the *Confessiones* in
which Augustine describes language learning.) These
maps are then tested against the manifold of experience. If they do their task -- if they bring order to

the chaos of experience, rendering it rational -- then
they are preserved. If they fail at their task then
they are modified or discarded. There are three tests
for ordering experience. First, a physical, empirical
test. Does the map allow the body to navigate in the
physical world? Second, a test for generalizability.
Do we recognize that the map can be applied to new encounters with the problematic data? Third, a valua-
tional test. As a consequence of the first two tests,
one ought to come to recognize that knowledge of the
principal ideas is the more important form of knowledge.

The third test, at first glance, seems other-
worldly. Actually, it is close to a form of aesthetic
preciousness. The beauties of serial music are in perception of the score, not in hearing the music. The
beauties of physics lie in appreciation of mathematical
proof, not in the explosion of the bomb or the stabil-
ity of the bridge. The beauties of architecture lie in
the blueprint, not in the building. Augustine recognizes that it is an idealization of design that we ap-
preciate. "In things constructed, a proportion of
parts that is faulty, without any compelling necessity,
unquestionably seems to inflect, as it were, a kind of
injury upon one's gaze." When something is well constructed it is obvious and "...need not be shown to
you in many words. In their own terminology, archi-
tects themselves call this design, and they say that
parts unsymmetrically placed are without design."[49]

Treating principal ideas cartographically preserves the independent existence of both map (principal
idea) and terrain (created things). It also avoids
Aquinas' interpretation of illumination as abstraction
from sense experience. Augustine explicitly states
that there are at least some sorts of knowledge (unity
or oneness) that cannot be abstracted from experience.

The cartographic model helps us to understand how illumination works and to see precisely the role that principal ideas play in the human conceptual scheme. We can come to form increasingly useful experience-structuring ideas as a consequence of examining provisional ideas and utilizing the ideas in new cases. In this non-theistic account, illumination becomes the procedure for formulating and testing ordering concepts.

Chapter 6

Footnotes

[1] For discussions of these and other positions see
Ronald Nash, *The Light of the Mind*, Kentucky, 1967,
Ch. 7 & 8 and Robert E. Buckenmeyer, "The Meaning of
Judicium and Its Relation to Illumination in The
Dialogues of Augustine," *Augustinian Studies*, Vol. I,
1970, p. 89.

[2] Ronald Nash, "St. Augustine on Man's Knowledge
of the Forms," *The New Scholasticism*, 1967, p. 230-231.

[3] *Intelligit quis in oriente justitiam: intelligit
alius in occidente justitiam...* IJE XXXV, 4.

[4] *...numquid alia est justitia quam ille intelligit,
alia quam iste?* IJE XXXV, 4.

[5] *...et dic mihi utrum inveniatur aliquid quod
omnes ratiocinantes sua quisque ratione atque mente
communiter videant...* DLA II, 8, 20.

[6] *...cum illud quod videtur praesto sit omnibus,
nec in usum eorum quibus praesto est commutetur...*
DLA II, 8, 20.

[7] *...sed incorruptum integrumque permaneat, sive
illi videant, sive non videant...* DLA II, 8, 20.

[8] *Separati sunt corpore, et in uno habent acies
mentium suarum.* IJE XXV, 4.

[9] *Habemus enim alium interioris hominis sensum isto
longe praestantiorem, quo justa et injusta sentimus:
justa, per intelligibilem speciem; injusta, per ejus
privationem.* DCD XI, 27, 2.

[10] *Ergo quoniam manifestum est esse te...* DLA II,
3, 7.

11
*Sunt namque ideae principales formae quaedam, vel
rationes rerum stabiles atque incommutabiles, quae
ipsae formatae non sunt, ac per hoc aeternae ac semper
eodem modo sese habentes, quae in divina intelligentia
continentur.* DDQ XLVI, 2.

12
*In illa igitur aeterna ceritate, ex que
temporalia facta sunt omnia, formam secundum quam
sumus, et secundum quam vel in nobis vel in corporibus
vera et recta ratione aliquid operamur, visu mentis
aspicimus...* DT IX, 7, 12.

13
*...utrum verum illud quod sine instrumento
corporis animus intuetur sit per seipsum, et non sit in
animo, aut possit esse sine animo.* DIA VI, 10.

14
*Si hoc loco esset ubi corpus nostrum est, non eam
videret qui hoc modo in Oriente de corporibus judicat.
Non ergo ista continentur loco; et cum adest ubicumque
judicanti, nusquam est per spatia locorum, et per
potentiam nusquam non est.* DVR XXXII, 60.

15
*Manent autem, non tanquam in spatiis locorum fixa
veluti corpora: sed in natura incorporali sic
intelligibilia praesto sunt mentis aspectibus, sicut
ista in locis visibilia vel contrectabilia corporis
sensibus.* DT XII, 14, 23.

16
*...nec peragitur tempore, nec migrat locis, nec
nocte intercipitur, nec umbra intercluditur, nec
sensibus corporis subjacet.* DLA II, 14, 38.

17
*...omnibus proxima est, omnibus sempiterna; nullo
loco est, nusquam deest; foris admonet, intus docet;
cernentes se commutat omnes in melius, a nullo in
deterius commutatur; nullus de illa judicat, nullus
sine illa judicat bene.* DLA II, 14, 38.

18
...in interiore homine habitat veritas. DVR
XXIX, 72.

19
*Ea vero quae intelliguntur, non quasi alibi posita
intelliguntur, quam ipse qui intelligit animus: simul
enim etiam intelliguntur non contineri loco.* DIA VI,
10.

20
*Anima vero negatur eas intueri posse, nisi
rationalis, ea sui parte quo excellit, id est ipsa mente
atque ratione, quasi quadam facie vel oculo suo
interiore atque intelligibili.* DDQ XLVI, 2.

21
*...quam illud mentis atque intelligentiae lumen,
quo et ista inferiora dijudicantur...* DGAL XXI, 24,
50.

22
*Et ea quidem ipsa rationalis anima non omnis et
quaelibet, sed quae sancta et pura fuerit, haec
asseritur illi visioni esse idonea: id est, quae illum
ipsum oculum quo videntur ista, sanum, et sincerum, et
similem his rebus quas videre intendit, habuerit.* DDQ
XLVI, 2.

23
...ut ratio sit quidam mentis aspectus... DQA
27, 53.

24
*Ratio est aspectus animi, quo per seipsum, non
per corpus verum inuetur...* DIA VI, 10.

25
*...aut ipsa veri contemplatio, non per corpus;
aut ipsum verum quod contemplatur.* DIA VI, 10.

26
*Quod autem intellectu capitur, intus apud animum
est: nec id habere quidquam est aliud, quam videre.*
DUC 13, 28.

27
*Minus ergo ea quae tangimus, vel quae gustamus,
vel quae olfacimus, huic sunt veritati similia, sed
magis ea quae audimus et cernimus: quia et omni
verbum a quibus auditur, totum auditur ab omnibus, et
simul a singulis totum; et species omnis quae oculis
adjacet, quanta videtur ab uno, tanta et ab alio
simul.* DLA II, 14, 38.

28
   ...sed simul omnibus tota est communis. DLA II, 14, 37.

29
   Nicolas Malebranche, tr. by Morris Ginsberg, *Dialogues on Metaphysics and Religion* (London and New York: Allen and Unwin, Ltd., 1923), Second Dialogue.

30
   ...nec ego de tua mente aliquid cerno, nec tu de mea... DLA II, 9, 27.

31
   ...quae in divina intelligentia continentur. DDQ XLVI, 2.

32
   Frederick Copleston, *A History of Philosophy* (Garden City: Image Books, 1953), Vol. II, Part I, Chapter 4.

33
   Quapropter nullo modo negaveris esse incommutabilem veritatem, haec omnia quae incommutabiliter vera sunt continentem; quam non possis dicere tuam vel meam, vel cujusquam hominis, sed omnibus incommutabilia vera cernentibus... DLA II, 12, 33.

34
   ...nobis in abdito mentis quarumdam rerum quasdam notitias... DT XIV, 7, 9.

35
   DT VII, 15, 24.

36
   Quoniam et quod de me scio, te mihi lucente scio; et quod de me nescio, tamdiu nescio, donec fiant tenebrae meae sicut meridies in vultu tuo. CO X, 5, 7.

37
   ...sic mens nostra, qui est oculus animae, nisi veritatis lumine radietur, et ab illo qui illuminat nec illuminatur, mirabiliter illustretur, nec ad sapientiam nec ad justitiam poterit pervenire. IJE XXXV, 3.

38
   Ipsumque lumen, quo cuncta ista discernimus, in quo nobis satis apparet quid credamus incognitum, quid cognitum teneamus, quam forman corporis recordemur, quam cogitatione fingamus, quid corporis sensus

attingat, quid imaginetur animus simile corporis, quid
certum et omnium corporum dissimillimum intelligentia
contempletur: hoc ergo lumen ubi haec concta dijudican-
tur, non utique, sicut hujus solis et cujusque corporei
luminis fulgor, per localia spatia circumquaque dif-
funditur, mentemque nostram quasi visibili candore
illustrat, sed invisibiliter et ineffabiliter, et tamen
intelligibiliter lucet, tamque nobis certum est, quam
nobis efficit certa quae secundum ipsum cuncta
conspicimus.   EP 120, 2, 10.

[39] *...verae atque incommutabiles sunt regulae*
numerorum, quorum rationem atque veritatem incommutabi-
liter atque communiter omnibus eam cernentibus...   DLA
II, 10, 29.

[40] *Nam etiam sol iste et videntis faciem illustrat,*
et caeci: ambo pariter stantes, et faciem ad solem
habentes illustrantur in carne, sed non ambo illuminan-
tur in acie; videt ille, ille non videt...   IJE XXXV,
4.

[41] *...quemadmodum oculos carnis videt quae in hac*
corporea luce circumadjacent, cujus lucis capax eique
congruens est creatus.   DT XII, 15, 24.

[42] *...sed lucem illam incorpoream contingere*
nequeunt, qua mens nostra quodammodo irradiatur, ut de
his omnibus recte judicare possimus.   Nam in quantum
eam capimus, in tantum id possumus.   DCD XI, 27, 2.

[43] *...sive in ipsa mentis luce veritate.   DT XIV,*
7, 9.

[44] *Ipsa vero forma inconcussae ac stabilis veritatis*
...eadem luce incorruptibilis sincerissimaeque...
imperturbabili aeterni tate perfundit.   DT IX, 6, 11.

[45] *...quoniam qui facit eam, venit ad lucem...   CO*
X, 1, 1.

[46]
Incorporalem substantiam scio esse sapientiam, et lumen esse in quo videntur quae oculis carnalibus non videntur... DT XV, 8, 14.

[47]
IJE XXV, 4.

[48]
DVR 29, 73.

[49]
Quippe in rebus fabricatis, nulla cogente necessitate iniqua dimensio partium facere ipsi aspectui velut quamdam vitetur injuriam...nec multis verbis vobis aperienta. Unde ipsi architecti jam suo verbo rationem ista vocant; et partes discorditer collocatas, dicunt non habere rationem. DO II, 11, 34.

Chapter 7
Understanding and Communication

For Augustine the characteristics that distinguish
human beings from the other animals are the human abilities to understand and to communicate that understanding. Animals live in the same physical environment we
live in. They, too, are able to survive in this environment. In fact, some of them sense certain kinds of
things more clearly than we can. Human beings, however, can do something more with their environment --
they can understand it. Up to this point we have
considered each element of Augustine's epistemology independently. An epistemology, however, must be unified.
Unity is especially important for a mentalistic epistemology, for it is a particular individuated thing -- a
mind -- that does the knowing. Thus, it is important
to consider what Augustine has to say about the faculties of understanding and judgment. We shall approach
this issue in two ways. Each approach will fill a
lacuna in the analysis to this point. First, we shall
consider the third element in the trinity of visions
mentioned in Chapter 5. The three visions are *visio
corporis*, *visio spiritualis*, and *visio intellectus*. In
our consideration of perception we saw that Augustine
utilized the first two visions in accounting for the
formation of a mental image which represents the physical world. In Chapter 6 we considered Augustine's

account of our access to principal ideas, the standards
that we use to judge the physical world. *Visio intellectus* is the faculty that judges mental images in
terms of principal ideas.

The second approach will involve a consideration
of the inner-faculties that we did not consider in
Chapter 5. In that chapter we were concerned to discuss inner-vision to the exclusion of the other senses
in the earlier discussion of the inner-man. These
other inner-faculties -- specifically, inner-speech and
hearing -- play a central role in thought and the communication of understanding.

I

Intellectual Vision

In Chapter 5, we considered the first half of
Augustine's trinity of visions. Referring to a half of
a trinity seems peculiar, but we saw that *visio spiritualis* could be taken in two different ways. One way
to take *visio spiritualis* -- animal sight -- renders it
an outer faculty which deals with the reports made by
the bodily senses in much the same way that animals
deal with such reports. Another way to take *visio
spiritualis* -- spiritual vision -- is to treat it as
the mental capacity that forms images based upon the
reports of the body's senses. I have also suggested a
view of Augustine's treatment of sensation that shows
how the spiritual vision knows what image to generate.
There remains one sort of vision to consider. It is
the vision that judges, and it is the vision that is
properly called "inner sight." I will explain the dif-
ferences that hold among intellectual, spiritual, animal and bodily visions and, in so doing, provide an
account of intellectual vision's special characteristics.

Intellectual vision is the most epistemologically important of Augustine's trinity of visions. It is a purely mental process, having no connection, either direct (as do bodily sight and animal vision) or indirect (as does spiritual vision), with the physical world. Augustine calls intellectual vision reason, understanding, and an intuition of the mind. Thus, it is "...the head or eye of the soul..."[1]

Intellectual vision can take two sorts of objects. "...{T}here are two kinds of knowable things: One, those things which the mind perceives by means of the bodily senses; the other, those which it perceives by itself."[2] The mind perceives material objects through the media of images formed by spiritual vision. Intellectual vision takes these images as its objects and by focusing on these images we learn about the world.

In explaining how it is that intellectual vision is aware of the images that are generated in spiritual vision Augustine tells us that the announcement which bodily sight makes to spiritual vision "...is also made to the intellect, which presides over the spirit."[3] The word it uses is *praesideo*, which means to oversee, preside, manage, direct, guard. *Praesideo* is a relationship that holds among all of the visions, spiritual vision or animal sight presiding over bodily sight, intellectual vision presiding over all the other visions. This is the key to Augustine's explanation of how intellectual vision recognizes when it is seeing an image of a present corporeal object. By being aware of the operation of both bodily sight and spiritual vision, intellectual vision is able to determine when the image it sees is to be associated with a material object.

Augustine also indicates that a rational soul "...with the mind understands those realities that are

neither bodies nor likenesses of bodies..."[4] These
"realities" are the principal ideas that are revealed
by illumination. They serve as standards for our judgment about all aspects of our experience. Intellectual
vision, then, is the faculty that learns *a priori*
truth, and it is the seat of our judgment of the material world.

> We do not make judgments concerning
> (other material objects) by our
> senses. For, we men have an other
> and far higher, perception which is
> interior, and by which we distin-
> guish what is just from what is
> unjust-justice by means of an intel-
> lectual form; what is unjust by lack
> of such a form.[5]

Intellectual vision uses one sort of mental object --
principal ideas -- to judge another sort of object --
material objects -- by means of a third sort of object
-- mental images. Intellectual vision, then, is that
sort of vision which distinguishes humans from other
animals. In transactions with the physical world, only
humans can get beyond appearances. We can learn what
is true about the physical world. Our judgments of
images in spiritual vision are made by appeal to principal ideas.

Intellectual vision provides both knowledge of
corporeal things, and, more importantly, what Augustine
calls "wisdom" and what we may call *a priori* knowledge.
Intellectual vision does not only make use of its special objects to understand the images created in animal
vision. It can also attend to principal ideas themselves. Just as corporeal things are available to a
glance of the bodily eye, so are these things at hand

to a glance of the mind (...*mentis aspectibus*...).
"...{A}s the eye of the flesh sees things adjacent to
itself in this bodily light..."[6] so does the eye of the
mind see its special objects.

What Augustine does with intellectual vision is
summarized as follows:

> Since thought is a kind of sight of
> the mind; whether those things are
> present which are seen also by the
> bodily eyes, or perceived by the
> other senses; or whether they are
> not present, but their likenesses
> are discerned by thought; or whether
> neither of these is the case, but
> things are thought of that are
> neither bodily things nor likenesses
> of bodily things, as the virtues and
> the vices; or as, indeed, thought
> itself is thought of; or whether it
> be those things which are the subjects
> or instruction and of liberal sciences;
> or whether the higher causes and rea-
> sons themselves of all these things in
> unchangeable nature are thought of; or
> whether it be even evil, and vain, and
> false things that we are thinking of,
> with either the sense not consenting,
> or erring in its consent.[7]

So, it is through the operation of intellectual vision
that we gain any and all of our knowledge.

II

Error

Up to this point I have confined myself to
Augustine's positive epistemology -- to his analysis of

how we come to know things. However, any well drawn
epistemology has to confront error -- mistaken judgment
-- sooner or later. All along in this study I have
maintained that a well drawn epistemology is present --
either implicitly or explicitly -- in Augustine's remarks on knowledge. There is something peculiar,
however, about his analysis of error; especially perceptual error.

On one hand the five "well-known messengers of the
body" -- the senses -- are passive faculties and, thus,
are not the sources of error (for they are not engaged
in active judgment). On the other hand, the active
faculty which judges -- *visio intellectus* -- seems to
be incorrigible[8] and, thus, cannot be the source of
error. Since this eliminates two obvious candidates it
is difficult to determine what Augustine thinks the
source of perceptual error is. I will argue that, contrary to the generally accepted view, Augustine must
take *visio intellectus* to be the source of error.

Augustine's most mature discussion of error is
found in *De Genesi ad Litteram* Book XII.

> However, the soul is deceived by the
> similarities of things, not through
> any fault of things, but through fault
> of the soul's supposition when, because
> of a deficiency of the intellect, it
> takes things which are similar (i.e.,
> it so takes things which are similar
> to *other* things). The soul is deceived
> in bodily vision when it supposes that
> what actually arises only in the bodily
> senses arises in things themselves, or
> when it supposes one thing to be some
> (other) thing which is of similar color,

or which sounds or tastes or feels
similar, or when the soul, having
been disturbed by sudden and unan-
ticipated bodily sights, supposes
that it is dreaming or supposes
that it is affected by a spiritual
vision in another way.[9]

Augustine begins his discussion of error with a
general statement of what he takes error to be. Mistaken belief seems to be exclusively the fault of the
believer, rather than the fault of whatever the objects
of belief are. Augustine anticipates Descartes in
maintaining that we are not deceived by objects when we
err but, rather, that we are deceived in our judgment
of objects in that we judge in terms of a standard of
which we have inadequate knowledge. Sometimes two different objects have a similarity. When we take one of
those objects to be the other, we judge inadequately.
The simple formula for error, on Augustine's account,
is: Taking one thing for another.[10]

Augustine considers specific conditions that would
serve to generate error in judgment based upon the testimony of the senses. His examples, familiar to contemporary readers, include stationary objects which
appear to move when viewed from moving vehicles and
oars in water which appear to be bent. According to
Augustine we make such errors in judgment because we
suppose that the things we are seeing have all of the
qualities that they *seem* to have. For example, a bent
oar is *similar* to an oar in water. We take one thing
to be something that is similar to it because the
images generated by the spiritual vision of a bent oar
and an oar in water are similar.

There is a second source of error in such judgments that is, again, familiar to contemporary readers.

In this second case I suppose that I am seeing one
object when, in fact, I am seeing a different object,
not because the object seen lacks a property which I
think it has, but because it has a property which is
similar to a property that a different object has.
Identifying the properties leads me to suppose that the
object is something other than it is. Again,
Augustine's examples are familiar: Thinking that a pot
of wax is a pot of beans; hearing the rumble of a cart
and supposing it to be thunder. This kind of mistake
highlights Augustine's assertion that the perceiver is
the sole source of error.[11]

Augustine's third source of error is not commonly
discussed by modern writers. In this case I see something that is so strange that I suppose I am dreaming
or hallucinating. We are more accustomed to dealing
with the problem just the other way around -- as when I
dream and suppose that I am awake. However, although
the contemporary epistemologist may be concerned with
Macbeth's dagger, which is seen even though it is not
there, Augustine is concerned with Siegmund's sword,
which is not seen even though it is there.

Augustine analysis of hallucinations and dreams
centers on *visio spiritualis* rather than *visio corporis*.
Again, we see that error is the taking of one thing for
another, but this time it is taking an image of an object to be the object itself. "Bodies themselves are
not in the mind at all when we conceive them, but only
their likenesses; thus when we take the latter for the
former we err..."[12] "In animal vision, that is, among
the likenesses which the mind sees, the mind is deceived when it judges those things seen in this way to
be bodies themselves..."[13]

But this is where the problem for our understanding of Augustine arises, for we may wonder just what it

is that errs in these latter kinds of error. Since
error is explained in terms of some inadequacy on the
part of the perceiver, the source of error in corporeal
matters (taken very broadly so as to include supposing
that a dream demon is a real demon, for example) ought
to be bodily sight, animal vision or intellectual vision. One or some combination of these would be the
likely candidate for the source of error in perception
because one or a combination of these is the source of
veridical experience.

     Let us consider each sort of error in bodily sight
first. In the bent-oar case what the bodily sight reports to the animal vision is a bent-oar-appearance.
It reports a bent-oar-appearance when the oar is bent
or (obviously) when the oar only seems to be bent.
Animal vision is required to generate an image. However, all that animal vision has to work with *vis a vis*
the *content* of the image it has generated is what the
bodily sight reports. And, the bodily sight reports
the raw, undifferentiated data of experience. It neither interprets nor structures that experience. So,
when the bodily sight reports a bent-oar-appearance a
bent-oar-image is produced. In the second case, when a
cart rumbles past, the bodily hearing reports an uninterpreted rumble-seeming to *visio spiritualis*.[14] In
the animal sight an image of rumbling is generated but
it is, again, uninterpreted. It is presented to the
intellectual vision as rumbling, not as cart-rumbling
or thunder-rumbling. The third case (supposing that a
genuine experience is a dream) is similar to the first
two cases, since a report of the body is again generated into an image in animal vision. Here, however,
there is no quality of the image to be mistaken. Thus,
neither bodily sight nor animal vision is the source of

error. The bodily sight accurately reports the state
of the corporeal world. The animal vision accurately
represents the report. The mistake is in our judging
that this accurate representation of the world is, in
fact, an hallucination or a dream. The judging faculty
is *visio intellectus*.

The second kind of error discussed above further
establishes intellectual vision as the source of error.
When I dream or hallucinate, bodily sight plays no role
at all. Images are generated in animal vision which
are not the result of reports from the bodily senses.
These images are taken to be reports about the corporeal world -- but they are not so taken by animal vision, since animal vision does not take anything to be
anything -- they are so taken by *visio intellectus*. It
is this highest faculty, then, that *must* be the source
of error in judging.

It is not only in judging the corporeal world that
we make mistakes. We also err when we judge whether an
act is just or a thing is beautiful or what the sum of
two and two is. Augustine discusses this kind of error
as well, error which involves principal ideas.

> ...In intellectual vision this {the
> soul} is not deceived; either it
> understands and...{what it understands}
> is true; or else if...{what it under-
> stands} is not true, it does not under-
> stand; thus, it is one thing to err in
> what the soul sees, and another thing
> to err because it does not see. [15]

One way to take this passage is to suppose that intellectual vision is in some sense incorrigible. It cannot be incorrigible when judging corporeal states of
affairs since it is the source of mistaken judgments in

corporeal matters. Augustine might hold that when
visio intellectus is attending to its proper objects
(eternal truths) it either sees them or it does not see
them, understanding when it sees, failing to understand
when it fails to see (rather than when it sees poorly).

There is reason to suppose that Augustine was prepared to grant incorrigibility to *visio intellectus* in
making some judgments: That I exist, for example, or
that I desire happiness. However, incorrigibility for
visio intellectus would seem to be ruled out by the
recognition that intellectual vision is the source of
error in judging the corporeal world and by the recognition that we can be mistaken in what we take to be
justice, beauty and so on. These sorts of knowledge
claims are independent of experience of the material
world. Unfortunately, this raises a problem for
Augustine. The analysis thus far -- that we err with
visio intellectus when we do not see what we think we
see -- does not tell us *why* we think we see what we
think we see.

Augustine suggests a solution to this difficulty
in *De Magistro*. He considers the process of learning
eternal truths, "Things...which we perceive through the
mind..."[16] Such things are inner and their understanding is essentially inner. Thus, the person who learns
does so through his own efforts of contemplation,
rather than through anything he is told, for he
"...knows of that which I speak by means of his own
contemplation, not through my words."[17] This analysis
is adequate for positive cases, when both teacher and
student agree immediately about what an eternal truth
is. But what happens when two people disagree about a
principal idea? At least one of them will be wrong,
and it is in dealing with this sort of case that we

would expect Augustine to come to grips with the
problem of error in our knowledge of eternal truths.

> Now if it often happens that the
> person questioned denies something,
> and is forced by other questions to
> affirm what he denies, this arises
> because of a defect in his vision
> in so far as he cannot consult that
> light about the whole affair. He
> is advised to do it part by part
> when he is questioned by one step
> after another about those very parts
> of which the whole consists, which
> he is unable to see as a whole.[18]

Visio intellectus errs in contemplating eternal truths,
then, when it takes a part of the truth to be the whole
truth. One need not put too much weight upon the notion of "part of the truth" in order to see Augustine's
point. His doctrine of illumination helps us to see
that the parts of eternal truths that are seen by the
erring inner-man are not portions of eternal truth but,
rather, qualities which eternal truths exhibit.

What Augustine intends here can best be understood
by considering an analogous case for seeing material
objects with physical sight. A poorly illumined object
will be seen, perhaps, as only an outline. As the illumination either increases in intensity or improves in
quality (for example, lighting the front surface of the
object rather than the top) more of its qualities become apparent. To return to intellectual vision, the
mistake made when we have an incorrect notion of an
eternal truth is to suppose that partially apprehending an eternal truth is apprehending a whole eternal
truth, and that apprehending an eternal truth wholly is
to apprehend all of its properties clearly.

Both understanding and being mistaken -- in all contexts -- are inner processes for Augustine. The analysis he offers for error (the taking of one thing for another) applies to all contexts. It is intellectual vision that judges correctly and incorrectly -- correctly when the judgment fits the rational superstructure of principal ideas, incorrectly when that superstructure is only partially known. Human beings are able to communicate both truth and falsehood to others, and Augustine's account of communication continues to utilize the inner-man metaphor.

III

The Inner Dialogue

Augustine's account of knowledge may be dominated by an interiority, but it is not solipsistic. In fact, he uses the inner/outer metaphor to explain how we are able to organize and then communicate what we learn. In particular, he writes of an inner-mouth[19] that is heard by an inner-ear.[20] What the inner-ear hears are inner-words or "speeches of the heart." To the objects of inner-vision, then, this cozy dialogue adds inner-words. However, Augustine warns us not to suppose that inner-speech and inner-sight are distinct operations for the inner-man.

> And yet, when we call thoughts speeches
> of the heart it doesn't follow that they
> are not also acts of sight, which arise
> from the sight of knowledge when they
> are true...For when they are done out-
> wardly by means of the body, then speech
> and sight are different things. But
> when we think inwardly, the two are one,
> just as sight and hearing are two things
> mutually distinct in the bodily senses.

> To see and to hear are the same
> thing in the mind. And thus, while
> speech is not seen but is rather
> heard outwardly, yet the inner
> speeches, that is, thoughts, are
> said by the Holy Gospel to have
> been seen, not heard, by the Lord.[21]

This equation of inner-speech and inner-sight is important for Augustine's philosophy of mind and epistemology. We have seen that he recognized that some operations of the mind are active while others are passive. He writes of bodily sight and hearing in terms of the objects they can take. Bodily speech does not take objects; it is intransitive. Inner-sight and hearing involve the registering or recording of thoughts, while inner-speech and outer-speech apply to the reporting of thoughts.

It is inner-speech that primarily concerns us here.[22] Inner-words have several unique characteristics. They are not the words of any natural language. The language which the inner-man speaks "...is neither Greek, nor Latin, nor of any other tongue,"[23] because it is "...before all diversity of languages."[24] In *Sermon* 187 Augustine explains how inner-words are related to outer-words (words expressed by the body, either through speech, writing, or gesture), and how inner-words are related to words of natural languages. (Outer-words, or words of natural languages, may be thought. When they are thought they are nonetheless outer-words.) Before a speaker or writer expresses his thought in a natural language the "...matter to be expressed exists bare and unadorned in the chambers of the heart..."[25] as inner words.

Inner-speech is temporally, logically and ontologically prior to outer-speech. The sense in which it

is temporally prior is discussed in several of his
sermons.

> ...{B}ehold, I who speak with you
> now, I thought in advance what I
> might say to you before I came to
> you. When I thought what I might
> say to you, there was already a
> word in my heart, for I would not
> speak to you without thinking
> beforehand. I found you to be a
> Latin speaker so I offered you a
> word which is Latin. However, if
> you were Greek I would have to
> speak Greek to you and offer you
> a Greek word. That word in my
> heart is neither Latin nor Greek,
> for what is in my heart is antece-
> dent to such languages. I search
> for a sound for it, I search for a
> vehicle as it were. I search for
> a means whereby it may reach you
> without leaving me.[26]

The above may be seen simply as an historical account
of Augustine's preparation of this sermon. He first
thought *about* what he was going to say, then he entered
his cathedral and said it. However, I think that there
is more to this passage than Augustine's assurance that
his sermons are not *ad lib*. Consider his remark about
expressing the inner-word as Latin or Greek as conditions warrant. The inner-word is what Augustine considers before speaking. It precedes any expression in
a natural language but the inner-word is not itself a
word of a natural language. Inner-words may not be
sounded in any way, nor may they be displayed in any

medium in which words of natural languages may be
displayed. An inner-word is a word "...which is neither utterable in sound nor capable of being thought
under the likeness of sound, such as must be the case
with words of any tongue."[27] This restriction applies
to inner-words when thought as well. One can think of
a word in a natural language as a sound or as a group-
ing of letters. Inner-words may not be thought of in
this way.

That Augustine thought of inner-words as temporally prior to outer-words is reinforced by two other passages: "...{T}hat which is brought forth in sound is
the same as that which before had been sounded in si-
lence...,"[28] and,

> Behold, I already know what I wish to
> say, I hold it in my heart, I seek the
> ministry of the voice; before I sound
> the utterance in my mouth I hold the
> word in my heart. Thus, the word pre-
> cedes my utterance and the word is in
> me earlier, the utterance is later.
> To you, in so far as you understand,
> the utterance first reaches your ears
> so that the word may be introduced to
> your heart.[29]

The outer word, then, is preceded by an inner-word.

However, if Augustine does mean to hold, literally,
that inner-words temporally precede their outer mani-
festations, rather than, for example, holding that
outer-speech can be contemporaneous with inner-speech,
then the inner-word/outer-word relationship becomes a
peculiar one. It becomes peculiar because it seems
contrary to even a primitive account of language. In
most cases it is simply not true that my outer-speech

is preceded by inner mutterings of some sort. In order
to see this we need only consider the phenomenon of
thinking out loud. In response, Augustine might hold
that we always do think inwardly before speaking and
that the criticism that we are not aware of such inner
mutterings is irrelevant, since we need not be aware of
such mutterings in any way other than by producing
outer-speech. An awareness of inner-speech just consists in the generation of outer-speech. However,
whatever his response, in the passage discussing the
generation of outer-speech Augustine is concerned to
raise other sorts of issues. Most importantly,
Augustine's insight consists in the following: We are
unable to introspect other minds but we can often come
to know what another person is thinking. We do this by
observing his behavior and by listening to what he has
to say. "For there is a hidden oracle there {the
inner-man} where it is hidden to men, we cannot hear
the mouth of the heart unless the mouth of the body
sounds with it."[30]   What a man thinks, then, must stand
in some peculiar relationship to what he says and does.

     What is this relationship and what is the nature
of the inner relatum?

     Augustine writes about communication because he
wants to explain how one mind can come to know another.
We communicate inner-words through out actions -- most
importantly, through outer-words. But, how reliably
can we communicate this information? At *De Magistro*
13,14 he gives us several reasons for *not* regarding
outer speech as revealing what a speaker is thinking.

     First, speech may not be good evidence for what a
person is thinking because the speaker may not know
what he is talking about. If he is ignorant about a
subject but is nonetheless holding forth concerning it,

then it follows that what he says is not what he thinks.
Secondly, when the speaker lies, what he says and what
he believes are by definition different. A third reason for distinguishing between thought and speech is
that the speaker may be reciting something which he has
memorized, for example, a hymn or a chant.[31] Finally,
what the outer voice says may be a slip of the tongue.

Unthinking speech and slips of the tongue are sug-
gestive examples. Unlike the other examples he uses
(ignorant speech, lying, and his fifth and sixth examples, idiosyncratic speech and speech which is not
heard correctly by the audience), slips of the tongue
and rote recitation are not conceptually tied to something going on in the mind of the speaker of which the
speaker must be aware. Ignorant speech is speaking
without knowing, rather than speaking without thinking.
When a person speaks from ignorance, whether to impress
or to avoid embarrassment, he thinks what he says, but
his thought is not founded in knowledge. In the case
of lying it is clear that the speaker thinks what he
says and believes that what he says is false. In the
case of idiosyncratic speech the speaker thinks what he
says, the problem is that he is using words in a
strange way, and thus, *we* cannot be sure about what he
is thinking. Finally, when we mis-hear, the speaker
thinks what he says, and says it; we just do not hear
it correctly. (I have, for the purposes of explanation, treated these classifications as mutually exclu-
sive.)

What is unique about rote recitation is that
nothing in particular has to be going on in the mind of
the reciter; he may be thinking about anything. What
is unique about slips of the tongue is that although
the speaker must be thinking something when he speaks,

what he thinks need not have any connection with what
he says. Peculiar to both of these is that internal-
izing them generates incoherent notions.

Unthinking outer-speech cannot become unthinking
inner-speech, since inner-speech is thought. Slips of
the inner-tongue should be impossible, since a slip of
the tongue is analyzable as: "I intended to say *P* but
I said something else." Since the inner-man does the
intending the inner-tongue does no slipping. To suppose otherwise is to invite the sort of regress which
always seems to be lurking in the background when we
use inner-man talk.

All of this points to an essential distinction between inner-speech, or thought, and outer-speech. It
is essential in that thinking out loud seems to be
ruled out, for outer-speech has certain peculiarities
which inner-speech lacks. The insistence that there is
a distinction between thought and speech is not a mistake. Indeed, in a passage that might be taken from an
introductory logic text, Augustine gives us another
reason to suppose that they are different:

> Between *Deum* and *Theon* there is a
> different sound. One word has these
> letters, another has those. However,
> in my heart, in what I wish to say,
> in what I think, there is no diversity
> of letters, no sound of various syl-
> lables. What is there is what it is.
> To say it to a Latin speaker, one
> utterance is applied, to a Greek
> speaker, another...to a Punic speaker
> another...to an Egyptian another...
> How many utterances may a word of the
> heart become without changing or
> varying itself?[32]

Thus, one very good reason for maintaining a distinction between inner and outer words is that inner-words may be brought forth in many different ways but no matter which natural language is used, the inner-word does not change. From the passage immediately above, it is unclear whether Augustine means for us to see that *his* inner-word remains unchanged no matter what language he is speaking, or that any speaker has the same inner-word no matter what natural language he may speak. The question of whether Augustine thought that all men speak the same inner-words is of some historical interest, as the answer to it might establish that Augustine had an embryonic version of Ockham's account of Mental Language. However, the doctrine of inner-speech involves more fundamental issues than this one.

Sometimes we know what someone is thinking on the basis of something he says. Speech is evidence for what the speaker thinks because inner-words stand in peculiar relationships to outer-words.

> ...{E}ven when one formulates a
> statement, although we utter no
> sound, yet because we think words
> we speak within the mind. And so
> in all speech we only remind.
> Words inhere in memory. We consider
> them, and this causes to come into
> the mind the very things of which
> words are signs.[33]

When we want to say something we first formulate in the mind the statement we want to make and then memory provides us with the correct outer words to use. Thought always precedes its expression. In order to find the right words to express the thought we have to search

our memories. In order to search our memories we have
to know what words of inner-speech we seek to express.
Thus, the sequence from inner-word to outer-word is:
inner-word; search of memory to find outer-words for
the inner-words; outer speech. But, granted that this
is an analysis of the generation of outer speech, one
question needs answering: How do we know which word to
select from memory so as to properly express our
thought?

Augustine deals with this question explicitly in
Book I of his *Confessiones*. In a famous passage he
tells us that he learned the meaning of words through a
kind of simple ostension.

> ...{M}y elders would make some
> particular sound, and as they made
> it would point at or move toward
> some particular thing. From this
> I came to realize that the thing
> was called by the sound they made
> when they wished to draw my atten-
> tion to it. That they intended
> this was clear from the motions of
> their bodies, by a kind of natural
> language common to all races which
> consists in facial expressions,
> glances of the eye, gestures, and
> the tones by which the voice ex-
> presses the mind's state...[34]

Unfortunately, this passage is famous because it has
been quoted by contemporary philosophers as an example
of an incorrect account of language learning. It is
claimed that only the simplest "language game" is
learned in this way, that anything so complex as a
natural language contains words that simply cannot be
defined through ostension.

I will not defend Augustine's notion of language
learning as simple ostension. I do think, however,
that for several reasons Augustine's account of how
words have meaning is not to be so easily dismissed as
it has been. Augustine's account of the role language
plays indicates a deeper understanding of meaning and
communication than is revealed by the passage quoted
immediately above. My strong claim is that Augustine
is far more sophisticated in his view of language than
he has been given credit for. My weak claim is that
Augustine does not have to be held to the simple ostension view, for there is a more sophisticated view of
language that is consistent with what he has to say
about the inner-man and his relationship to the corporeal world.

The analysis I have been proposing of Augustine's
inner-man will help us to understand some of
Augustine's views of language.

In Chapter 6 of Book I of the *Confessiones*
Augustine describes his growing consciousness of the
world during his childhood.

> ...{G}radually I began to notice where
> I was, and the will grew in me to make
> my wants known to those who might sat-
> isfy them; but I could not, for my wants
> were within me and those others were
> outside, nor had they any faculty
> enabling them to enter into my mind.[35]

Augustine observes that an infant does not understand
why his wants are not fulfilled and, thus, the infant
flies into a rage when his message is not received. In
order to make his inner wants known he has to communicate them to others, and the desire to communicate has
an inner source.

> ...I have since discovered by
> observation how I learned to speak.
> I did not learn by elders teaching
> me words in any systematic way...
> But of my own motion, using the
> mind which You, my God, gave me I
> strove with cries and various sounds
> and much moving of my limbs to utter
> the feelings of my heart -- all this
> in order to get my own way.[36]

In order to deal with the corporeal world we have to
communicate our needs to others. There is a parallel
that may be drawn here between Augustine's account of
language learning and the discussion of Augustine's
theory of perception in Chapter 5.

The inner-man must be aware of the state of the
material world, so the spiritual vision generates
images of that world. The inner-man sometimes has
needs and desires that require action on the part of
others. Unfortunately, minds only have access to other
minds through the services of bodies. Thus, the inner-
man must learn the public names of objects, whether the
objects are material objects or principal ideas. Generally, the correct outer-word is chosen for the same
reason that the spiritual vision generates the correct
image; it is necessary for the continued existence of
the individual that he learn how to deal with the material world. Thus, inner-words may be brought forth as
outer-words and as bodily actions.

Inner-speech is not only temporally prior to
outer-speech, it is also logically prior. In order for
words of outer-speech to have sense there must be
inner-words associated with them. As we have seen,
this does not mean that words uttered thoughtlessly or

by rote will have no meaning. It *does* mean that outer-words will lack sense if they are associated with no one's inner-words.

Inner-words are also ontologically prior to outer-words. It is the inner-word that is the real word. The only reason the outer-word has any meaning, and the only reason we call an outer-word "word," is because it is "begotten" by the inner-word. In the absence of this relationship to an inner-word, an outer-word is only meaningless noise.

The Use of Inner-Speech

Augustine uses inner-speech to explain how we deal with bits of knowledge that we have learned and how we come to perform bodily actions.[37]

Communication:

One important kind of bodily action is the "bringing forth" of inner-words as outer-words, words in a medium which is available to the senses of others. We communicate in inner-word to another through speech or gesture. "...{A} word which we bear in our mind may become known also by bodily signs to the bodily senses."[38] Since we do not have access to other minds it is necessary for us to express our thoughts in media which can be made available to other bodies. Thus, we speak or we write. Outer-speech and outer-writing suffer a distinct disadvantage, however. They are not thought "...as it really is, but rather, as it can be seen or heard by the body."[39] This disadvantage is not shared by inner-speech, since inner-speech is knowledge "...spoken inwardly as it really is."[40] There is a numerical difference between knowledge and inner-speech, but when we say something which is true (this is literally what Augustine says, I think that what he means is when we say something honestly) then "...what

is in the knowledge is in that {inner-word} and what is
not in knowledge is also not in that {inner-word}."[41]

When we want someone else to know something that
we know, or when we want someone else to do something,
we signify (*significare*) the inner-word with an outer
sign (*signum*). Although the principal means of communication is speech, we may communicate as well through
writing. "...{L}etters have been invented so that we
may be able to converse also with those who are absent.
But these are signs of words, as words are signs in our
conversation of those things we think."[42] Written
words, then, are signs for spoken words, and spoken
words are signs for things that we think.[43] In fact,
thoughts are the real words. "...{T}he word that
sounds outwardly is a sign of the word that gives light
inwardly. The latter has greater claim to being called
a word."[44] That is, we call what the bodily voice ut-
ters "a word," but it is, in fact, the sound of a word
(...*vox verbi*...). Inner-words may not be represented
in any medium which may be used to represent sounds.
However, a sound may be intimately associated with an
inner-word, so intimately associated that (*ceteris
paribus*) another person hearing the sound (and knowing
the conventional association of outer-word to inner-
word) will come to have the same inner-word that the
speaker has. Despite this occasional intimate association, there remains an essential difference between
inner-words and outer-words. "For, when it (the inner-
word) is uttered by sound, or by any bodily sign, it is
not uttered as it really is, but as it can be seen or
heard by the body."[45] How, then, are inner-words com-
municated by outer words if they are so essentially
different? To explain this phenomenon Augustine re-
minds us that God was able to make himself known to

men by utilizing a medium which was essentially
different from His own. God had to express His Word in
some medium which would be available to the bodily
senses. Thus, we are told, the Word of God was made
flesh. Similarly, we must make our inner-words available to the senses of others.

One important similarity between God's method for
expressing His desires and man's method for doing the
same involves what it is that is actually being made
available to the bodily senses. When God (or His Word)
was made flesh, it was not God Himself who was made
flesh. God was not manifested in a material medium to
the senses of men. Rather, it was God's creation that
was made available in a material medium. In the case
of inner-words being brought forth, the inner-word is
not changed into an articulate sound. Rather, it assumes (*ad sumere*) an articulate sound.

> ...the word which we form within us
> becomes an utterance when we bring
> it forth from our mouth. The word
> is not changed into the utterance
> but the voice by which it comes forth
> is taken on while the inner-word re-
> mains unchanged. What is thought
> remains within, what is heard sounds
> forth.[46]

An inner-word which is expressed as an outer-word does
not cease to exist when it is expressed. It is not
consumed (*consumere*) by the outer-word. It is not
transformed into an articulate sound. The inner-word
continues to exist as, and even after, the outer-word
is spoken.

Thought:

Augustine explicitly suggests that a useful way to
treat knowledge is to deal with it as though it were

words that we speak (or "have") within us. "We behold,
then, by the sight of the mind...the form...We have
true knowledge of things which are then conceived, as
it were, as a word within us..." [47] Summarizing the relationships that hold among knowledge, memory, inner
and outer words, Augustine maintains that

> All these things, then, those which
> the human mind knows by itself, those
> which it knows by the bodily senses,
> and those which it knows and has gained
> through the testimony of others, are
> placed and saved in the storehouse of
> memory. And from these is generated a
> word that is true when we say that we
> know, and a word that is prior to all
> sound, prior to all thought of sound.
> For it is when a word is generated by
> memory that it is most similar to some-
> thing that is known. Such a word
> belongs to no language, and is a true
> word about something which is true.
> All that such a word is is derived
> from that knowledge which generates it.
> Such a word does not indicate when the
> person who speaks what he knows learned
> what he knows, for sometimes a person
> may speak something he has just learned.
> All of this is true about such a word,
> provided only that the word itself is
> true, that is, sprung from knowledge. [48]

     Known things are of three sorts. There are things
that the mind comes to know by itself. "...realities
that are neither bodies nor the likenesses of
bodies..." [49] These are the principal ideas. There are

as well those sorts of things that are known through
the bodily senses. The third sort of known thing
echoes those images in animal vision which Augustine
calls fictitious images, images which are "...fashioned
by the power of thought..."[50]

Whenever we say something that we know, an inner-
word is generated by known things.

> ...when we speak what is true, that
> is, speak what we know, there is
> born from the knowledge itself, which
> the memory retains, a word that is
> totally of the same kind as the knowl-
> edge from which it is born. For the
> thought that is formed by the thing
> we know, is the word which we speak
> in the heart...[51]

Augustine might have maintained that when we say
something that we know, the inner-word which is stored
in memory then generates an outer-word, but he does not
write of knowledge as though it were inner-words which
are stored. Instead, he appeals to proto- and
primitive linguistic talk only when he wants to explain
a mental operation which involves knowledge, when he
wants to describe how it is that we are able to let
someone else know something that we know, that is, when
he gives an analysis of true assertions. When we say
something true, the inner-word which assumes an outer-
word predicates certain properties. Whatever these
properties are, they are due only to the knowledge
being expressed.

Knowledge is intimately associated with inner-
words, but it is not the same as inner-words.
Augustine explains the relationship between knowledge
and inner-words by saying that knowledge "begets"

(*gignere*) the inner-word. "A word is then (when we speak what we know) most like the thing known..."[52] How this happens is explained in *De Trinitate*.

> The true word comes into existence
> when, as I said, that which we toss
> to and fro by revolving it comes to
> that which we know, and is formed
> by that in taking its entire likeness.
> So that in whatever manner each thing
> is known, in that manner it is also
> thought, that is, said in the heart...[53]

We consider various possibilities stored in memory before coming upon something that we know, and that thing which is stored in memory, which we know, then forms an inner-word.

We recognize a familiar Augustinian device in his use of inner-speech. Generating knowledge claims involves a trinity. There is something that is stored in memory. This generates or begets an inner-word which in its turn is brought forth as an outer-word.

VI

The Roles of Inner-Sight and Inner-Speech

Augustine recognizes that sometimes the mind passively records or examines what it experiences, other times it actively creates or reflects upon its experiences. Inner-sight takes as objects either things which are generated in animal sight or things which are located in the mind itself. When Augustine talks about how it is that we gain knowledge he appeals to talk about inner-sight. However, when Augustine is concerned to explain how it is that we tell someone else something that we know he deals with mental processes as though they were inner-speech.

The similarities between his account of gaining knowledge and his account of reporting knowledge

become even more striking when we compare the processes
which Augustine supposes are involved. When we see
something in the corporeal realm an image is generated
by spiritual vision. It is then presented to inner-
vision. When we want to express something we know, an
inner-word is created from something stored in memory.
It is then brought forth as an outer-word. The expression of knowledge, in fact, is easier to explain for
Augustine than is the acquisition of knowledge of the
material world, since there is no difficulty involving
inferior things having some effect on superior things.

V

Evaluation

We understand and we communicate that understanding. Both understanding and communication are governed
by strictly pragmatic considerations. These considerations provide both the impetus for the particular
operations and the means for their successful accom-
plishment. I shall say nothing more about Augustine's
account of communication. However, some aspects of his
theory of understanding bear scrutiny.

How are we to evaluate his account of intellectual
vision? We may begin by considering the means we would
use to evaluate any account of judgment.

Judgment is supposed to accomplish one thing; it
is supposed to provide us with the truth. Thus, we
evaluate *any* account of understanding by seeing
whether, above everything else, it gives us truth. If
it does, we may go on the apply other tests. Does it
give us the truth more efficiently (more directly) than
any alternatives (where alternatives are those cognitive systems that give us the same truth)? Is the
truth provided in a systematic way? Does the cognitive
system work predictably (does it always give us the

truth)? If the account of understanding does not give
us the truth, then (of course) concern with these
other questions would be absurd.

At this point we encounter one of the central difficulties of epistemology. We are trying to determine
whether a system of judgment is a good one; we are trying to judge whether that system judges well. What
standards of judgment are we to apply? Is Augustine's
account of understanding a good one? In terms of what?

All along I have been arguing that there is no absolute truth "out there" which exists over and above
our best efforts to find the truth. At one level, this
is not a position that Augustine would have been sympa-
thetic toward. It is clear that he maintained the
truth of authority -- the teachings of his faith -- to
be the truth against which the result of reason must be
measured. Just as clearly, however, there is an
Augustine who tried to gain as much knowledge through
reason as he could. This, obviously, has been the
Augustine I have been writing about. This Augustine
does not reject the teachings of pagan philosophers out
of hand, because such teachings may give us truth. A
spoiling of the Egyptians is acceptable -- in fact,
desirable -- because non-Christian thought may be helpful to understanding. This Augustine seems to be governed by one central motive: Does it work? If it
does, keep it. If it does not, keep looking.

It is this motive that gives us the basics for
judging Augustine's view of understanding, for a pragmatic test is one that can be applied to any cognitive
system. In fact, a stronger claim can be made, for a
pragmatic test seems to be the only one that can be applied to a cognitive system without either undermining
the system itself or begging the question. Suppose

that one argued that a system of judgment S must meet
the criteria of some other system T before we accept S
as being an adequate mode of judgment. To argue this
would be to give supremacy to T as a system of judgment.
Thus, S would cease to be the important cognitive system (at least, for epistemologists); T would become the
standard system of judgment; T would have to be justified; and, either we would be back where we began *or* a
regress would ensue. Alternatively, if we wish to
maintain that S is the ultimate system of judgment, we
shall have to take S as the standard of its own justification, and this begs the question. What is left?
We may determine whether or not the system works.

In all aspects of Augustine's epistemology we have
encountered this pragmatic element, and it will be apparent to anyone familiar with the Pragmatists that the
argument offered above is a traditional pragmatic argument. Epistemologists recognize two sorts of knowledge:
particular knowledge and general knowledge. Particular
knowledge is knowledge appropriate to discrete circumstances, it is knowledge which is applicable to individuals. General knowledge is applicable to classes of
things, it is appropriate to the realm of reason. This
distinction is sometimes taken to be the theoretical/
practical distinction, but as we shall see this is not
quite correct.

The distinction between general and particular
knowledge may not be drawn with sharp borders. For one
thing, we hold each to be answerable to the other.
When we formulate a general account of the world --
what I have been calling a map -- this general account
must apply to particular circumstances. If it does
not, then it is modified until it does (or until it is
rejected or is changed so radically as to be a

different account). When we have particular experiences
-- when we survey, to continue the map metaphor -- these
experiences are expected to be consistent with the general account of the world. If they are not, we are inclined to reexamine the experienced situation rather
than modify the general account (save in cases in which
the dissonance between the experience and the general
account results from an experience so strong that we
cannot reject it). Use reflects the map, but sometimes
the map must be modified as a consequence of use.
Which, then, takes precedence?

Mapping is not done on whim. There is purpose behind it. A conscious, rational decision has been made
to map this particular area, rather than that. The same
is true of the general aspects of a cognitive system.
Those general views are not arrived at randomly, they
are formed for a purpose. Once again, there is a pragmatic impetus in beginning the process of concept formation and testing.

We have seen that Augustine recognizes this process. He also seems to give precedence to the resultant
map.

> ...it is possible for there to be
> science without practice, and very
> frequently greater science than in
> those who excel in practice; but
> on the other hand they can't even
> acquire practice without science.[54]

This means that the general picture of the world
("science") is necessary before the particular elements
of the world ("practice") can be confronted. Human
beings cannot engage the particular aspects of the
world without a "likely story," without a general picture of what the world is like. Contrary to the

received empiricist account human knowledge is not the
result of random marks on a *tabula rasa*. It is, rather, an active, creative process.

Chapter 7

Footnotes

1
...*animae nostrae caput aut oculum...* DLA II, 6, 13.

2
...*duo sint genera rerum quae sciuntur, unum earum quae per sensus corporis percipit animus, alterum earum quae per se ipsum...* DT XV, 12, 21.

3
...*etiam intellectui nuntiatur, qui et spiritui praesidet...* DGAL XII, 11, 22.

4
...*sive cum mente intelliguntur, quae nec corpora sunt, nec similitudines corporum...* DGAL XII, 24, 51.

5
Sed nosse ea sensu corporis ita capimus, ut de his non sensu corporis judicemus. Habemus enim alium interioris hominis sensum isto longe praestantiorem, quo justa et injusta sentimus: justa per intelligibilem speciem; injusta per ejus privationem. DCD XI, 27, 2.

6
...*oculos carnis videt quae in nac corporea luce circumadjacent...* DT XII, 15, 24.

7
Quandoquidem cogitatio visio est animi quaedam, sive adsint ea quae oculis quoque corporalibus videantur, vel caeteris sentiantur sensibus, sive non adsint, et eorum similitudines cogitatione cernantur; sive nihil eorum, sed ea cogitentur quae nec corporalium similitudines, sicut virtutes et citia, sicut ipsa denique cogitatio cogitatur; sive illa quae per disciplinas traduntur liberalesque doctrinas; sive istorum omnium causae superiores atque rationes in natura immutabili cogitentur; sive etiam mala et vana, ac falsa cogitemus, vel non consentiente sensu, vel errante consensu. DT XV, 9, 16.

[8]
For example, Vernon Bourke, *Augustine's Quest of Wisdom*, Bruce Publishing Company, Milwaukee, 1945, p. 244.

[9]
Illuditur aetem anima similitudinibus rerum, non earum vitio, sed opinionis suae, cum approbat quae similia sunt pro iis quibus similia sunt, ab intelligentia deficiens. Fallitur ergo in visione corporali, cum in ipsis corporibus fieri putat quod fit in corporis sensibus...aut cum putat aliquid hoc esse, quod similiter coloratum est, vel similiter sonat, vel elet, vel sapit, vel tangitur...aut cum repentinis inopinatisque corporalibus visis anima turbata vel in somnis videre se putat, vel aliquo hujusmodi spirituali viso affici... DGAL XII, 25, 52. A similar discussion may be found in Plato's *Thaetetus*, 187E-190E.

[10]
Presumably, the similarity in terms of which the error is made may be a real or an imagined one. However, if it is only an imagined similarity it looks as though error may be explained in terms of further error -- mistakenly thinking that there is a similarity between two objects when there is none.

[11]
In his earliest discussion of error, in *Contra Academicos* and in *Soliloquia*, Augustine's analysis depended upon false objects as the source of mistakes. He soon came to realize the difficulties of this view, particularly as an analysis of perceptual error. (For example, it seems clear that when I see a false object I am seeing something and attributing correct properties to it.)

[12]
...non enim omnino ipsa corpora in animo sunt, cum ea cogitamus; sed eorum similitudines; itaque cum eas pro illis approbamus, erramus... DT IX, 11, 16.

[13]
In visione autem spirituali, id est in corporum similitudinibus, quae spiritu videntur, fallitur anima,

cum ea quae sic videt, ipsa corpora esse arbitratur...
DGAL XII, 25, 52.

[14] Remember that *Visio Spiritualis* plays a role in all the bodily senses.

[15] *...in illis intellectualibus visis non fallitur: aut enim intelligit, et verum est; aut si verum non est, non intelligit: unde aliud est in his arrare quae videt, aliud ideo errare quia non videt.* DGAL XII, 25, 52.

[16] *Cum vero de iis agitur quae mente conspicimus...* DMA 12, 40.

[17] *...novit quod dico sua contemplatione, non verbis meis.* DMA 12, 40.

[18] *Nam quod saepe contingit, ut interrogatus aliquid neget, atque ad id fatendum aliis interrogationibus urgeatur, fit hoc imbecillitate cernentis qui de re tota illam lucem consulere non potest quod ut partibus faciat, admonetur, cum de iisdem istis partibus inter- rogatur, quibus illa summa constat, quam totam cernere non valebat.* DMA 12, 40.

[19] DC I, 2.

[20] DC II, 4.

[21] *Nec tamen quia dicimus locutiones cordis esse cogitationes, ideo non sunt etiam visiones exortae de notitiae visionibus, quando verae sunt. Foris enim cum per corpus haec fiunt, aliud est locutio, aliud visio: intus autem cum cogitamus, utrumque unum est. Sicut auditio et visio duo quaedam sunt inter se distantia in sensibus corporis, in animo autem non est aliud atque aliud videre et audire: ac per hoc cum locutio foris non videatur, sed potius audiatur, locutiones tamen interiores, hoc est, cogitationes*

visas dixit a Domino sanctum Evangelium, non auditas...
DT XV, 10, 18.

[22] One might attempt an analysis of inner-speech
which is analogous to Augustine's analysis of outer
speech. Such an analysis may be profitable in certain
respects, for example, in clarifying the relationship
between speech and the objects of speech. But outer
speech is a case of expressing physically a sign of
one's will, and inner-speech is not a case of expressing a sign of one's will. In fact, it is questionable
whether the words of inner-speech are signs at all.
When discussing praying aloud, at *De Magistro* I, 2,
Augustine says, "For he who speaks expresses the sign
of his will by means of articulate sound. But God
should be sought and entreated in the very secret
places of the rational soul, which is called the inner-
man..." Thus, when we pray we are speaking with our
inner-mouth. But, if that's what God attends to when
he hears our prayers, is the inner-mouth then expressing *signs*?

[23] *...quod nec graecum est, nec latinum, nec linguae
alicujus alterius...* DT XV, 10, 19.

[24] *...ante omnem linguarum diversitatem...* SE 187,
3.

[25] *...adhuc in cubili cordis quodam modo nuda est
intelligenti...* SE 187, 3.

[26]*...ecce ego qui vobiscum loquor, antequam ad vos
venirem, cogitavi ante quod vobis dicerem. Quando
cogitavi quod vobis dicerem, jam in corde meo verbum
erat. Non enim vobis dicerem, nisi ante cogitarem.
Inveni te Latinum, latinum tibi proferendum est verbum.
Si autem Graecum esses, graece tibi loqui deberem, et
proferre ad te verbum graecum. Illud verbum in corde*

*nec latinum est, nec graecum; prorsus antecedit linguas
istas quod est in corde meo. Quaero illi sonum, quaero
quasi vehiculum; quaero unde perveniat ad te, quando non
recedit a me. SE 225, 3.*
[27]
*...quod neque prolativum est in sono, neque
cogitativum in similitudine soni, quod alicujus linguae
esse necesse sit... DT XV, 11, 20.*
[28]
*...hos idem tamen profertur in sono, quod ante
sumuerat in silentio... SE 187, 3, 3.*
[29]
*Ecce jam scio quod volo dicere, corde teneo
ministerium vocis inquiro; antequam sonet vox in ore
meo, jam tenetur verbum in corde meo. Praecessit ergo
verbum vocem meam, et in me prius est verbum, posterior
vox: ad te autem, ut intelligas, prior venit vox auri
tuae, ut verbum insinuetur menti tuae. SE 288, 4.*
[30]
*Obscurum enim responsum ibi, ubi homines latet,
qui os cordis, nisi os corporis consonet, audire non
possunt. DME 16, 31.*
[31]
A similar point is made at DT XIII, 20, 26.
[32]
*Inter Deum et Theon distat sonus; literae aliae
sunt hic, aliae sunt ibi; in corde autem meo, in eo
quod volo dicere, in eo quod cogito, nulla est
diversitas litterarum, nullus sonus varius syllabarum;
hoc est quod est. Ut enuntiaretur Latino, alia vox
adhibita est; ut Graeco alia so Punico...aliam...
Hebraeo, aliam...Aegyptio, aliam...Indo, aliam. Quam
multas voces faceret personarum mutatione verbum cordis, sine ulla sui mutatione vel varietate? SE 288, 3.*
[33]
*...simul enim te credo animadvertere, etiamso
quisquam contendat, quamvis nullum edamus sonum, tamen
quia ipsa verba cogitamus, nos intus apud animum loqui,
sic quoque locutione nihil aliud agere quam commonere,*

*cum memoria cui verba inhaerent, ea revolverdo facit
venire in mentem res ipsas quarum signa sunt verba.*
DMA I, 2.
34
   *...cum ipsa appelabant rem aliquam, et cum secun-
dum eam vocem corpus ad aliquid movebant, videbam et
tenebam hoc ab eis vocari rem illam, quod sonabant, cum
eam vellent ostendere. Hoc autem eos velle ex motu
corporis aperiebatur, tanquam verbis naturalibus omnium
gentium, quae fiunt viltu et nutu oculorus caeterorum-
que membrorum actu, et sonitu vocis indicante affec-
tionem animi, in petendis, habendis, rejiciendis,
fugiendisve rebus. CO I, 8, 13.*
35
   *Et ecce paulatim sentiebam ubi essem, et volunta-
tes meas volebam ostendere eis per quos implerentur,
et non poteram; quia illae intus erant, foris autem
illi, nec ullo suo sensu valebant introire in animam
meam. CO I, 6, 8.*
36
   *Et memini hoc; et unde loqui didicerim post
adverti. Non enim docebant me majores homines prae-
bentes mihi verba certo aliquo ordine doctrinae, sicut
paulo post litteras: sed ego ipse mente quam dedisti
mihi, Deus meus, cum gemitibus et vocibus variis, et
variis membrorum motibus edere vellem sensa cordis mei
ut voluntati pareretur, nec valerem quae volebam
omnia... CO I, 8, 13.*
37
   It seems to be implicit that an inner-word is not
neutral. A word of inner thought is such that when it
is brought forth, either by generating an outer word or
by bringing about some bodily action, the outer word or
the bodily action will be either right or sinful. "A
word is brought forth (born) when, thinking it out, it
pleases us either to sin or to do right." (*Nascitur
autem verbum, cum excogitatum placet, aut ad peccandum,
aut ad recte faciendum. DT IX, 8, 13.*)

One must not suppose that this commits Augustine to
the view that *x* will only count as a word of inner-
speech if it leads to right or sinful action. For one
thing, the characterization seems to be conditional:
If the word is brought forth, then such and such will
follow. Further, this particular passage seems to be
describing the conditions under which we would say that
a word of inner-speech had been successfully brought
forth as a word of outer speech. If this is correct,
then the view that there are no neutral inner-words
would be reinforced, unless Augustine holds that
neutral inner words cannot give rise to action.

In short, all inner words *may* give rise to outer
words or to bodily action. An inner-word is "brought
forth" when it somehow leads us to sin or to behave
correctly. So, words of inner-speech are not neutral.

We might here appeal to the Augustinian view that
there are no neutral states for man; that man is either
fallen or saved. If he is fallen, then when an inner-
word is brought forth it will lead him to sin (or, it
will be sinful). In *De Utilitate Credendi* II,
Augustine seems to be arguing for something like this.

[38]
  DT XV, 10, 19.

[39]
  ...*non dicitur sicuti est, sed sicut potest
videri audirive per corpus.*   DT XV, 11, 20.

[40]
  ...*quando eadem scientia intus dicitur, sicuti
est.* DT XV, 11, 20.

[41]
  ...*ut quod est in ista, hoc sit in illo; quod non
est in ista, non sit et in illo...*   DT XV, 11, 20.

[42]
  DT XV, 10, 19.

[43]
  This is one view of Augustine's analysis of the
relationship between written and spoken words. There
is some reason to believe that Augustine also thought

of written words as signs for inner-words. At IJE
XVIII, 8, Augustine explains that when written words
are generated they are first written "in the heart" and
then are written with the hand. The inner letters and
the outer letters are the same, although they are
formed differently. The heart forms them "intelligibly"
and the hand forms them visibly. Again, it is the context that saves Augustine, for in this book of IJE he
is discussing the way in which Christ was able to perform only those actions which God first performed.
Thus, rather than being a passage about how words come
to be formed, it is, instead, a passage about how the
inner-man anticipates outer actions. This time the
metaphor is being used to show us that intentional
actions are preceded by actions of the heart.

[44]
*Proinde verbum quod foris sonat, signum est verbi
quod intus lucet, cui magis verbi competit nomen.* DT
XV, 11, 20.

[45]
*Nam quando per sonum dicitur, vel per aliquid
corporale signum, non dicitur sicuti est, sed sicut
potest videri audirive per corpus.* DT XV, 11, 20.

[46]
*Sicut verbum quod corde gestamus, fit vox cum id
ore proferimus; non tamen illud in hanc commutatur, sed
illo integro ista in qua procedat assumitur, ut et
intus maneat quod intelligatur, et foris sonet quod
audiatur.* SE 187, 3.

[47]
*...visu mentis aspicimus: atque inde conceptam
rerum ceracem notitian, tanquam verbum apud nos
habemus...* DT IX, 7, 12.

[48]
*Haec igitur omnia, et quae per se ipsum, et quae
per sensus sui corporis, et quae testimoniis aliorum
percepta scit animus humanus, thesauro memoriae condita
tenet, ex quibus gignitur verbum verum, quando quod*

scimus loquimur, sed verbum ante omnem sonum ante omnem
cogitationem soni. Tunc enim est verbum simillimum rei
notae, de qua gignitur et imago ejus, quoniam de
visione scientiae visio cogitationis exoritur, quod est
verbum linguae nullius, verbum verum de re vera, nihil
de suo habens, sed totum de illa scientia de qua
nascitur. Nec interest quando id didicerit, qui quod
scit loquitur; aliquando enim statim ut discit, hoc
dicit; dum tamen verbum sit verum, id est, de notis
rebus exortum. DT XV, 12, 22.

[49] *Puto enim non inconguenter medium dici, quod*
corpus quidem non est, sed simile est corporis, inter
illud quod vere corpus est, et illud quod nec corpus
est, nec simile corporis. DGAL XII, 24, 51.

[50] *...seu fictas, sicut cogitatio formare potuerit.*
DGAL XII, 6, 15.

[51] *Necesse est enim cum verum lonquimur, id est,*
quod scimus loquimur, ex ipsa scientia quam memoria
tenemus, nascatur verbum quod ejusmodi sit omnino,
cujusmodi est illa scientia de qua nascitur. Formata
quippe cogitatio ab ea re quam scimus, verbum est quod
in corde dicimus... DT XV, 10, 19.

[52] *Tunc enim est verbum simillimum rei notae...*
DT XV, 12, 22.

[53] *Et tunc fit verum verbum, quando illud quod nos*
dixi volubili motione jactare, ad id quod scimus
pervenit, atque inde formatur, ejus omnimodam, simili-
tudinem capiens; ut quomodo res quaeque scitur, sic
etiam cogitetus, id est, ...in corde dicatur. DT XV,
15, 25.

[54] *...fieri quidem posse, ut scientia sine usu sit,*
et major plerumque quam est in eis qui usu excellunt;
sed tamen etiam illos ad usum tantum non potuisse sine
ulla scientia pervenire. DMU I, 5, 10.

Chapter 8
Augustine and Idealism

Every aspect of Augustine's epistemology has now been examined. This concluding chapter has two goals. When I introduced the inner-man locutions, I suggested that they constitute a particular kind of explanatory device for his epistemology. Having examined the epistemology, I will now return to a consideration of the inner-man in order to determine if it has served as a vehicle for explanation. This is a secondary goal for this chapter. There is a more important task.

As I have written about Augustine's account of knowledge, an underlying conceptual scheme has emerged. In this chapter I will make that scheme explicit. I will also attempt to conceptually locate Augustine in the history of epistemology.

The Inner-Man Considered

When I reviewed Augustine's use of the inner-man locutions earlier, I demonstrated that they appear in embryonic form in his earlier works. As Augustine's epistemology develops, this set of metaphors increases in sophistication and complexity. Augustine makes most extensive use of the inner-man locutions in his account of thought, especially when he discusses *a priori* truth. There are several reasons for his use of these locutions. Augustine may feel comfortable using inner-speech locutions to talk about thought because of the frequency of Biblical allusions to thought as being speech-like. For example, when Jesus heals the paralyzed man and forgives him his sins, the scribes "said within themselves" (Matthew 4:2-4), or the scribes and the pharisees "began to think, saying" (Luke 5:21-22) that Jesus had blasphemed. Such locutions abound in Scripture, and Augustine treats the Bible as central to human knowledge. However, I do not believe that Augustine uses inner-speech locutions when writing about thought merely because the Bible uses them.[1] Rather, Augustine uses such locutions because he is a teacher as well as a Christian. He recognizes that the mind and mental phenomena in general are difficult matters to discuss because we are not able to point to anything when we talk about them. Thus, when trying to tell someone about mental phenomena we use modes of speech and writing that permit us to appeal to something within the experience of our audience.

When Augustine wishes to discuss a subject which is extremely complex he will frequently draw analogies to a more familiar phenomenon. There are a number of different ways this may be done. One of the most useful is the analogue model. When I introduced the inner-man locutions at the outset of this investigation I suggested that they may be profitably analyzed in ways that are appropriate to the evaluation of such models. It is now time to so evaluate them.

Augustine's Use of the Inner-Man

Augustine recognizes that difficult matters may often be clarified by using ways of speaking that do not literally state the truth. Such ways of speaking are useful because "ambiguous things are more readily understood through analogies..."[2] Augustine also recognizes the dangers inherent in using analogies.

"...Be careful that you do not take figurative
locutions to be literal."[3]   "...We must not suppose
that it is necessary that what is signified by an analogy in one place must always be signified by that analogy."[4]   "There is not a visible thing that can be made
(to stand) in perfect harmony to an invisible thing."[5]

In explaining knowledge, Augustine recognizes that
he must give a clear, plausible account of the human
mind. He notes that philosophers have found the mind
to be especially difficult to understand. Some think
that the mind is

> ...the blood, others think it is
> the brain, others think it is the
> (physical) heart...others have
> thought that it is made of minute
> and individual particles, which
> they call atoms...Others have said
> that it is air, others that its
> substance is fire...Others have
> thought that it is nothing material
> at all...[6]

Augustine does not think that the mind is material,[7]
but he indicates that a very useful way to write about
the mind is to use language normally reserved for discussions of material objects.

> And because of that order of our
> condition through which we are made
> to be mortal and material, we can
> deal with visible things more
> familiarly than with conceptual
> things...And we must make our dis-
> cussion suit this incapacity, so
> that if we want to distinguish more
> adequately and accommodate inner and

spiritual things, we must choose
examples of analogies from outer
things applying to the body.[8]

So, Augustine recognizes the pitfalls as well as
the strengths of analogy when used to explain, and he
also recognizes that the difficult problem of describing mental phenomena may be simplified by use of a particular analogy, *viz.*, writing about the mind as though
it were a material thing.

We saw that Augustine used the inner-man locutions
to explain all areas of his epistemology. His primary
use for this metaphor was in his account of *a priori*
knowledge. However, there are some important secondary
uses as well.

When the inner-man locutions are used in what I
have called the primary or dominant case, to explain
our knowledge of *a priori* truths and to give some content to our relationship(s) to God, I think that the
inner-man serves as the set of analogies that make a
man's body in a physical environment a representational
analogue model. When the inner-man locutions are used
to explicate other matters, I am inclined to think that
Augustine uses inner-man talk because it is convenient.
In such cases he uses inner-man talk because it is
available and because it permits him to connect his
epistemology to his other views. I shall briefly discuss the secondary cases first, and then concentrate on
the dominant case.

A brief review of the secondary uses of inner-man
talk will reveal an important common characteristic:
They all require interpretation and expansion in order
to produce an account with any degree of philosophical
sophistication. Probably the most obvious example of
this was Augustine's account of communication. The

problem of the inner-man, trapped in a body,
communicating with some other inaccessible inner-man,
trapped in another body, seems to have had some appeal
for Augustine. Interestingly, his account of communication amounts to a reversal of his account of learning
about corporeal objects. In this context the interplay
between inner-sight and inner-speech is important.
Inner-sight is the mental function central to learning.
Inner-speech is essential to reporting what was learned.
In communication, however, Augustine left unexplained
how the inner-voice generates the correct inner-word
which may then be spoken. My suggestion is that vital
attention guarantees the correct choice of inner-words.
I think this is the most fortuitous account that can be
given consistent with his other views. The analysis is
a pragmatic one, depending upon the view that it is the
task of the rational soul to preserve the body.

In the context of his discussion of perception the
inner-man locutions work fairly well because his account of how we know the material world is closest to
his account of how we know principal ideas -- and this
latter is the dominant case for his use of inner-man
locutions.

I am inclined to think that Augustine uses inner-
man locutions to deal with these secondary problems because he wishes to relate them to the heart of his
epistemology -- the theory of illumination; the way in
which humans are related to God.

The Dominant Case

Augustine's account of *a priori* knowledge must explain how we can have such knowledge and it must also
preserve the peculiar characteristics of such knowledge. Augustine's picture of the mind as a man inside
conjoined with his doctrine of illumination constitute

an explanatory device that serves these two tasks. The
explanatory device has as (important) primitive terms
"inner-man" and "principal ideas" (or *species*, *formae*,
eternal truths). Principal ideas are treated as special kinds of objects that have properties which are
co-extensive with the crucial characteristics of the
kind of knowledge Augustine wishes to account for.
Principal ideas are unchanging and are unchanged by
being known, they are private[9] but are "seen" by many
(but not all) human minds. Further, principal ideas
may be potentially "seen" by everyone. In using language that is normally applied to the body to explain
the mind Augustine employs the same technique that he
used in his discussion of *a priori* knowledge, explaining a mysterious phenomenon by appealing to a commonplace experience. In the context of his illumination
theory, he wrote of lights and material objects, in his
talk of mental phenomena he writes of a human body.
The dominant use for Augustine's inner-man locutions
ties his talk about the mind to his analysis of *a
priori* knowledge.

Evaluation of the Inner-Man

How does inner-man talk aid in understanding *a
priori* knowledge? In evaluating Augustine's inner-man
locutions we must first determine the exact status of
such locutions. The central strength of an analogue
model is that it enables us to understand a mystery by
drawing analogies between the mystery and something
that is commonplace. If we consider the material
realm, we see that it is a man's body and material objects and suns and lamps that are commonplace. The
mystery is not the inner-man, it is rather, man's (apparent) ability to have certainty about particular
facts. The inner-man, then, is a middle man, neither

commonplace nor mysterious, and it is this odd status
of the inner-man that must be remembered when evaluating him.

How well do the inner-man locutions do the job I
have suggested Augustine has in mind? In the discussion of models in Chapter 2, we saw that there are two
sorts of criteria that may be applied. Present tense
criteria, criteria in terms of which a model may be
chosen, and past tense criteria, criteria which are applied to a model after it has been developed.

Present Tense Criteria Applied

In his discussion of *a priori* knowledge Augustine
must meet the requirements of a diverse audience. His
audience will determine the criteria in terms of which
he will choose his explanatory model. Often Augustine
is addressing ordinary people, as when he delivers a
sermon. In these contexts the common ground he has to
draw on are Scriptural phrases such as "said in the
heart," or "said within themselves." Augustine also
addresses his fellow scholars. For example, early versions of *De Trinitate* were apparently circulated among
the scholars of North Africa. Here the common ground
is platonism, although not necessarily an extensive
knowledge of Plato. Augustine himself appears to have
been familiar with segments of *Meno*, *Timaeus* and
Phaedo, Plotinus' *Enneads* and, through Cicero's
Hortensius, with Socrates' thought. Scholars in such a
tradition would feel comfortable with the treatment of
necessary truths as being objects that have a special
ontological status. For both his audiences, then,
Augustine designs an epistemic picture which can be
treated on several levels.

Past Tense Criteria Applied

There are some difficulties raised for Augustine
by his utilization of inner-man talk. I have already

indicated that Augustine recognized the problems
inherent in explaining an unobservable phenomenon by
appeal to an observable one.

There is a second problem generated by surplus
meaning. Whereas in the material world there are both
sources of light and objects that reflect light, both
of which may serve as the proper objects of the bodily
sight, in the God/man world there are apparently only
sources of light. It seems that what permits the
inner-eye to see what it contemplates when it contemplates principal ideas is some power provided by the
ideas themselves, since it is the principal ideas' il-
luminating the mind that leads to understanding. This
does not strike me as a critical problem, since
Augustine simply points out that principal ideas may be
treated as lamps, as sources of light and as observable
objects themselves.

There is a more difficult problem generated by
Augustine's inclination to occasionally treat the
images attended to by the inner-eye as being inner-
words -- by his treatment of inner-sight and inner-
hearing as though they were co-extensive. In Chapter 4
we considered Augustine's description of the role
played by inner-vision when one thinks of a material
object which one has never seen. Augustine has never
seen Alexandria. Whenever he thinks about Alexandria[10]
the qualities of Alexandria represented by the image he
forms are based upon the testimony of others. This is
not the case with his thought of Carthage, for he has
visited Carthage and he thus has an image of Carthage
stored in his memory which depends upon the testimony
of his bodily senses for the qualities it has.
Augustine analyzes the role played by the reports of
others in forming both his image of Alexandria and the

related inner-word "Alexandria." He compares this to
the role played by his bodily senses in forming his
image of Carthage. If I want to think of Carthage I
first search my memory until I find my notion or image
of Carthage. The inner-word for Carthage and the image
of Carthage come to the same thing.

I do not suggest that Augustine thinks of inner-
words as being the same as images stored in memory.
Inner-words and images in memory are not *things* at all
for Augustine. They are ways of talking which permit
Augustine to explain, on one hand, how he is able to
remember anything about Carthage, and on the other, how
he is able to tell someone else what he knows about
Carthage. Further, Augustine does not use images and
inner-words as two different ways of speaking of the
same thing: he does not hold that thought is *essentially* linguistic and/or imaginal. For Augustine, when
we talk about thought, we can talk about it *as though
it were* linguistic.

Augustine searches for a means of explanation, of
course, because he supposes that there is *a priori*
knowledge and that knowledge always takes objects of
one sort or another. When we apply past tense criteria
to a model we must, I think, hold in check our criticism of the view that the model is intended to explain.
In this case, Augustine's problem must be taken seriously; we must suppose that there is a kind of knowledge that is puzzling.

Augustine's approach to this puzzle is to treat the
sort of knowledge he considers, knowledge *a priori*, as
though it were a different sort of knowledge, perceptual knowledge. He justifies so treating such knowledge on grounds that there are properties and
relationships shared by both sorts of knowledge (they

share a calculus). By extension, his treatment of
principal ideas provides him a way to demonstrate how
such ideas are used.

Principal ideas serve as standards for judgment.
This is probably their most important role. They serve
as standards for judgment about the material world
(whether, for example, something is beautiful), as
standards for judgment about human action (whether a
particular action is just), and as guidelines for behavior (whether something ought to be done). We gain
access to these principal ideas through illumination
(just as we can come to know about trees because the
sun shines on them) and we can learn about these ideas
through reflection and introspection (just as we can
learn about trees by looking at them more closely).
Inner-man locutions provide an account which helps explain how *a priori* truths work. Such locutions also
hint at ways in which a further understanding of *a
priori* truth may be gained.

Inner-man talk in Augustine's work is not *descriptive* of a model that helps us to understand his account
of knowledge *a priori*. Augustine does not advance a
homunculus view of the mind as an explanation of such
knowledge. Rather, Augustine's inner-man locutions
describe a set of analogies that make a man's body and
physical environment an analogue model for the human
mind and its relation to the mind of God. For
Augustine, then, the inner-man locutions constitute the
calculus that a man's body and its environment shares
with a man's mind and its relation to God's mind.

Of what consequence is this interpretation for our
understanding of Augustine's thought? If Augustine
literally takes the inner-man to be descriptive of a
man's mind, then this is sufficient evidence for

holding that Augustine is a metaphysical dualist.
However, if we characterize the inner-man as a purely
descriptive or heuristic device (not unlike ping-pong
balls and mouse-traps as explanatory of atomic reac-
tions) then the inner-man talk will not serve as evidence for such dualism. In much the way that we know
that there are electrons, we know that we have a peculiar relationship with God's mind because Augustine has
a theory that explains puzzling phenomena, and a central element in this theory is the peculiar God/man relationship.

The ultimate justification for Augustine's use of
inner-man locutions, and for his dualism, is that both
lead to an understanding of a puzzling phenomenon.
This is to suggest that they work. Augustine's talk of
an inner-man is neither naive nor does it incorporate a
primitive mistake.

Concluding Analysis

Several themes have emerged in my presentation of
Augustine's epistemology. In this section my goal is
to unify those themes and to provide an analysis of the
unity that relates Augustine to recent developments in
epistemology. The emergent themes are: Augustine's
interiority, the central role of memory, his active
theory of sensation, the treatment of *a priori* truths
as map-like, and Augustine's rationality, with all of
its conjuncts: system, structure, goals, purpose, and
so on.

Interiority: I have commented at length on the
sense in which Augustine's inner-man is an explanatory
device. Augustine did *not* look upon the inner/outer
dichotomy as a description of the world. There is
another aspect of Augustine's interiority that has
emerged but about which I have not commented: the

sense in which Augustine's interiority guarantees a
conceptual scheme that is mind-centered. It is important to emphasize at the outset that I am not arguing
that the interiority is evidence for dualism.
Augustine's dualism has never been an issue. He believes that there are minds and there are bodies. The
point here is that Augustine is offering a powerful
form of dualism, one that explains a series of phenomena that would otherwise be puzzling.

We have seen that the interiority of Augustine's
epistemology is not the simple "turning inward" that it
has been thought to be. The inner nature of knowledge
is more complex, amounting to the recognition that
knowledge requires both microscopic and macroscopic
structure. There is a localized structuring within
each specific area of Augustine's epistemology. Each
area, in turn, fits into a whole which itself is structured. Only a mind can accomplish this structuring.
Thus, interiority is not subjectivity. (One might make
the same point by seeing that the subjective/objective
distinction is an interior distinction. Objective
judgments being those that reflect the overall structure, subjective judgments being those that either do
not fit the structure *or* for which the whole story is
not known.)

The turning inward is not an indication that
Augustine took the proper objects of knowledge to be
inner-truths. Neither does it indicate a rejection of
the physical world. Augustine recognizes that nothing
can be understood -- known -- without a structure. He
also recognizes that this structure can only be imposed
by a structuring mind. Thus, for any sort of knowledge,
the important processes occur in the mind.

Memory: Memory becomes interesting when an epistemologist tries to get along without it. Augustine

recognizes that memory is essential to knowledge. If
memory doesn't work or cannot be justified, then the
rest of knowledge collapses. Some philosophers would
maintain that memory is a transcendental.

In Augustine's view the justification for memory
is that it works. In attempts to justify a memory
claim we saw that the only bases were generally reputable historical evidence. However, this is not to say
that memory is justified only by appeal to things that
have happened in the past. In fact, Augustine recognizes the present-tense nature of memory. I remember
ϕ. I know that this memory is reliable because it fits
with my other memories, ψ and Δ. At this point the
traditional regress problem is encountered, for ψ and Δ
must be known to be true if they are to serve as the
justification for ϕ. One way to respond to this would
be to seek a further series of propositions that would
justify ψ and Δ in the same way that ψ and Δ justified
ϕ. There is an alternative response that might be
given. Suppose that I engage in a task that utilizes
ϕ, ψ and Δ and I successfully completed that task.
Success becomes the measure of my remembering correctly.
Indeed success or purpose is a mark that distinguishes
rational animals from beasts.[11]

In considering his remarks on memory Augustine's
overall picture began to emerge. He is advancing a
pragmatically grounded Idealism. We accept generally
reputable historical evidence because such evidence
gives us the best chance of being right. What makes it
reputable is that it works. Things fit together. What
is shown by one sort of evidence is also shown by another. In the absence of such agreement we do not
know.

Sensation: We know of the material world only because the mind orders perceptions out of the forest of

bodily sensations. The mental images that are the
media for knowledge of the material world represent
that world. These images have certain qualities that
result from an active intervention of the mind. This
structuring gives Augustine something of a coherence
picture of sensation, but it is a coherence picture
that incorporates independent tests. These tests include the unified nature of the reports of the various
senses and the reports of other human beings.

I suggested that the Augustinian notion of "vital
attention" could be seen as a pragmatic dialectic. If
it were not an anachronism we might say that Augustine
is advancing a cognitive Darwinism.[12] The evidence
that human beings are able to successfully structure
their experiences may be found in the continued existence of human beings. If we were unable to structure
experience we wouldn't survive. We wouldn't survive
because we would not be able to safely interact with
the world. This is the consideration that governs
Augustine's pragmatic dialectic. His kinship with recent philosophers may also be seen by considering the
ontological status of material objects in his conceptual scheme.

Augustine expresses a view of the existence of
material objects that anticipates the Absolute Idealist
position of the Nineteenth Century. Material objects
owe their *existence* to the existence of a perceiving
mind.

>   And to whatever extent the things
>   which are inferior exist, they
>   exist because the form in which
>   they exist is given to them by
>   those more powerful than they...[13]

This is because material objects must be structured in
order to exist. "A corporeal object has some concord

between its parts, otherwise it could not exist at
all."[14] This structure is provided by the mind.
"...no body is made except by receiving its form from
the soul."[15] When a material object is judged on aesthetic grounds, it is this structure which provides the
basis of the judgment. "What is beauty of the body? A
harmony of parts with a certain pleasing color."[16]
Structure is *essentially* tied to reason. "...when we
behold something formed with well-fitting parts...we
say that it appears reasonably {fashioned}."[17]

Thus, the mind not only constructs physical objects
out of the manifold of experience, it also judges in
terms of this structure. There is more to Augustine's
treatment of physical objects than an antique version
of Absolute Idealism, however.

Augustine's treatment of material objects differs
in an important respect from the Idealist position of
the last century. We have seen that Augustine thinks
knowledge of the physical world is possible. He also
thinks that it is important.

> Far be it from us to doubt the truth
> of those things which we have perceived
> through the senses of the body. For
> through them we have learned of the
> heavens and the earth, and those things
> in them which are known to us...[18]

Perception does not only provide us with knowledge of
present material objects (the things that are the immediate objects of the bodily sight), it also provides
us with the basis for knowledge of other things. In
De Quantitate Animae Augustine discusses inferential
knowledge of material objects. We are able to infer
fire from seeing smoke. Thus, on the basis of experiencing one thing we can come to know about something

else. We can go beyond the immediate reports of
vision.[19]

So, these mental constructs are not fictions; they
make a difference, and the difference they make, as we
have seen, is tied to the continuing survival of the
body.

A Priori Knowledge: There are many knowledge
claims that seem in important respects to be independent of the reports of the senses. Augustine holds
that these special kinds of knowledge are a consequence
of our having a special kind of relationship to God's
mind. Through illumination human minds come to know
the principal ideas which provide the rational structure to the human conceptual scheme. Gaining access to
these ideas and applying them is an active human process. In explaining this process I introduced the map
metaphor.

Mapping reflects the utility of principal ideas.
This utility is aimed in two directions. First, a map
is not made unless it is useful. Its use will determine the properties that the map has, but its creation
is a response to need. Second, a map is preserved because it is useful. Ontologically, then, a map owes
its genesis and its continued existence to utility. On
the non-theistic analysis principal ideas are needed
because they order the crucial phenomena -- the
experiences confronted by the mind. These ideas are
central to the epistemology because they provide the
needed structure and order to all areas of human knowledge. Considering them within Augustine's explicit
system, it is easy to see why they provide this order:
The world is created by God in tune with these ideas.
But at this point we can make the important connection
of rationality and the creation of the world.

Rationality: At *De Vera Religione* 36,66 Augustine
ties the rationality of the created world to its creation by God. God created the world in accord with His
Divine Ideas. Thus, the world fits together, it is coherent and rational. When we perceive the world our
minds create a rational representation of the world.
Thus, *our* rationality is an essential element in understanding the created world because that world was
created by another rationality. And what is our rationality? Augustine has many things to say about reason,
but to my mind the most important remark he makes (and
the remark that best reflects the central theme of this
study) is "...a purposeful act is characteristic of a
rational animal."[20] Order is the general characteristic
of the human arts.[21] Thus, purpose and order are tied
to reason and -- more importantly -- these are tied to
the external world. To speak of purposeful human activity and to speak of the order inherent in the arts
is to speak of a physical manifestation of a mental phenomenon. Here, again, Augustine anticipates contemporary usage. When we judge that a person is rational we
judge on the basis of order and structure. *Of course*
it is possible to be wrong in both cases. A highly irrational person may appear to be acting rationally.
(Imagine someone peacefully reading Proust in a living
room in front of a warming fireplace. The image of
rational repose -- until we discover that there is a
tidal wave coming and the peaceful reader knows it.)
Highly ordered phenomena do not always entail rational
structure. (The ordering of stalactites and stalag-
mites in a cave, for example.) The point is that rationality means *at least* purpose, order and structure,
and the cases collapse only when we learn more. (A
final point: It is clearly possible that irrational

behavior be, in fact, highly rational, as when playing
with a child or, for that matter, with a lover.)

So, we see that rationality for Augustine is evi-
denced by order and purpose. The activity of reason,
however, involves more.

Reason is the faculty of analysis and synthesis.
"Analyze" and "synthesize" are common words. Often absent in their use, however, is a precise definition of
these processes. Augustine is clear in providing a
specific goal for both analysis and synthesis. It is a
unified conceptual scheme. "...both in analyzing and
in synthesizing, it is oneness I seek..."[22] This pursuit of unity is governed by the preconceptions of the
unity-imposing mind. "...when I analyze, I seek a
homogeneous unit; when I synthesize, I look for an in-
tegral unit. In the former case, foreign elements are
avoided; in the latter, proper elements are conjoined
to form something united and perfect."[23] This notion
of unification is also central to Augustine's remarks
about "consistent and convincing evidence," in *De
Trinitate*.[24]

The central characteristics of rationality are the
evidentiary characteristics of order and reason, the
instrumental characteristics of analysis and synthesis,
and the teleological characteristics of unity. All of
these characteristics work in harmony to construct a
workable conceptual scheme out of the disorder of sensation.

It may seem at this concluding point that wrench-
ing this epistemological view out of Augustine does
unjustifiable violence to his position. The view is,
after all, a non-theistic one and, although Augustine's
richness has generated an enormous number of interpretations, nobody has suggested that he is not a theist.

I do not suggest this, either. My suggestion is less direct. Augustine was certain that human minds could gain the truth simply by recognizing the correctness of the Christian Faith. In that regard, everybody had the potential to succeed. But, Augustine also recognized that God had given man reason, and that reason could also serve as a path to truth. That reason could accomplish this with a minimum of theistic explanatory support ought to be seen as being indicative of the power of reason and the magnificence of God's creation.

Chapter 8

Footnotes

[1] At DT X, 7, 9 Augustine reviews attempts that
have been made by philosophers to determine which part
of the human body the soul or the mind is. Of course,
Augustine's point here is to argue that the mind is
nothing corporeal and that philosophers who have
thought that it was were in error. In the process of
explicating the various notions (of other philosophers)
he is careful to differentiate the view that the mind
is the heart from the various Biblical passages that
mention the heart as being that which praises or loves
God.

"And, so some think that it is the blood, others the
brain, others the heart; not, as Scripture says, 'I
shall praise you, O Lord, with all my heart', and 'You
will love the Lord, your God, with all your heart', for
this word, by misapplication (*abundo*) or figurative use
(*transfero*) is drawn from the body to the soul..."
(*Itaque alii sanguinem, allicerebrum, alii cor, non
sicut Scriptura dicit, 'Confitebor tibi, Domine, in
toto corde meo', et 'Diliges Dominum Deum tuum ex toto
corde tuo', hoc enim abutendo vel transferendo vocabu-
lum ducitur a corpore ad animam. DT X, 7, 9.*)

I suspect that Augustine may be making this point to
head off a potential accusation of heresy. In this
section he argues against the view that the physical
heart is the soul. However, it looks as though there
is scriptural support for the view he is arguing
against. Thus, Augustine is very careful to indicate
that when the heart is mentioned in such contexts the
use is somehow unusual. It is unusual in a special
way: instead of its usual application to the body, it
is misapplied or transferred to the soul. Thus, there

is good reason to suppose that Augustine recognizes the
metaphorical nature of Biblical inner-man locutions.

[2]
*...nemo ambigit, et per similitudines libentius
quaeque cognosci...* DDC II, 6, 8.

[3]
*...cavendem est ne figuratam locutionem ad
litteram accipias.* DDC III, 5, 9; cf. CME III, 10, 24.

[4]
*...non putemus esse praescriptum ut quod in
aliquo loco res aliqua per similitudinem significaver-
it, hoc eam semper significare credamus.* DDC III, 25,
35.

[5]
*Non enim ulla visibilis similitudo invisibili rei
potest ad omnem convenientiam coaptari.* DLA II, 11,
32.

[6]
*Itaque alii sanguinem, alii cerbrum, alii cor...
Alii ex minutissimis individuisque corpusculis, quas
atomos dicunt...Alii acrem, alii ignem substantiam ejus
esse dixerunt. Alii eam nullam esse substantiam, quia
nisi corpus nullam substantiam poterant cogitare...*
DT X, 7, 9.

[7]
DT X, 7, 9.

[8]
*Et illo ipso ordine conditionis nostrae quo mor-
tales atque cornales effecti sumus, facilius et quasi
familiarius visibilia quam intelligibilia pertractamus
...Cujus aegritudini congruendum est: ut si quando
interiora spiritualia accomodatius distingere atque
facilius insinuare conamur, de corporalibus exterioribus similitudinum documenta capiamus.* DT X, 1, 1. I
shall resist the temptation to treat *ordine conditionis
nostrae* as "forms of life."

[9]
Malebranche's objection to locating Principal
Ideas in God's mind (*Dialogues on Metaphysics and
Religion*) and the subsequent treatment of Principal

Ideas as being "ideogenetic" complicate the analysis of such ideas, but I do not think the problem is relevant to the current discussion.

[10] DT VIII, 6, 9.

[11] DO II, 11, 33.

[12] Consider Nicholas Rescher, *Methodological Pragmatism*, Basil Blackwell (Oxford, 1977) Chapter VIII and Donald T. Campbell, "Evolutionary Epistemology," in *The Philosophy of Karl Popper*, ed. Paul A. Schilpp, Open Court (La Salle, 1974), p. 413.

[13] *Eoque sunt quae infirmiora sunt, in quantum sunt, quod species eis, qua sint a potentioribus traditur...* DIA XVI, 25.

[14] *Habet corpus quamdam pacem suae formar sine qua prerus nihil esset.* DVR II, 21.

[15] *Corpus enim nullum fit, nisi accipiendo per animam speciem.* DIA XVI, 25.

[16] *Quid est corporis pulchritudo? Congruentia partium cum quandam coloris suavitate.* EP 3, 4.

[17] *Itaque, cum aliquid videmus congruentibus sibi partibus figuratum, non absurde dicimus rationabiliter apparere.* DO II, 11, 32.

[18] *Sed absit a nobis ut ea quae per sensus corporis didicimus, vera esse dubitemus: per eos quippe didicimus coelumet terram, et ea qui in eis nota sunt nobis.* DT XV, 12, 21.

[19] DQA 24, 25.

[20] *...id autem est rationalis animantis factum propter aliquem finem.* DO II, 11, 33.

[21] DO II, 11, 34.

[22]
Ergo et in discernendo et in connectendo, unum
volo...   DO II, 18, 48.

[23]
Sed cum discerno; purgatum; cum connecto,
integrum volo.   In illa parte vitantur aliena, in hac
propria copulantur, ut unum aliquid perfectum fiat.
DO II, 18, 48.

[24]
DT XV, 12, 22.

Appendix

Chart of Abbreviations

    This list includes the abbreviation I use for each of Augustine's works, the Latin Title, an English translation of the Title, and the volume of Migne's *Patrologiae Cursus Completus, Series Latina* which contains the work.

CA – *Contra Academicos* (Against the Academics), PL 32.

CM – *Contra Mendacium* (Against Lying), PL 40.

CO – *Confessiones* (Confessions), PL 32.

DBV – *De Beata Vita* (The Happy Life), PL 32.

DC – *De Continentia* (On Continence), PL 40.

DCD – *De Civitate Dei* (The City of God), PL 41.

DDC – *De Doctrina Christiana* (On Christian Doctrine), PL 34.

DDQ – *De Diversis Quaestionibus* LXXXVI (86 Diverse Questions), PL 40.

DGAL – *De Genesi ad Litteram* (Literal Commentary on Genesis), PL 34.

DGCM – *De Genesi Contra Manichaeos* (On Genesis Against the Manichees), PL 34.

DIA – *De Immoralitate Animae* (Immortality of the Soul), PL 32.

DLA – *De Libero Arbitrio* (On Free Choice), PL 32.

DMA – *De Magistro* (Concerning the Teacher), PL 32.

DME – *De Mendacio* (On Lying), PL 40.

DMU – *De Musica* (On Music), PL 32.

DO – *De Ordine* (On Order), PL 32.

DQA – *De Quantitate Animae* (Magnitude of the Soul), PL 32.

DSD – *De Sermone Domini in Monte* (On the Lord's Sermon on the Mount), PL 34.

DSEL – *De Spiritu et Littera* (The Spirit and the Letter), PL 44.

DT - *De Trinitate* (On the Trinity), PL 42.

DUC - *De Utilitate Credendi* (On the Value of Believing),
       PL 42.

DVR - *De Vera Religione* (On the True Religion), PL 34.

EP - *Epistolae* (Letters), PL 33.

IJE - *In Johannis Evangelium* (On the Gospel of John),
       PL 35.

RE - *Retractiones* (Reconsiderations), PL 32.

SE - *Sermones* (Sermons), PL 38.

SO - *Soliloquia* (Soliloquies), PL 32.

Index

Texts and Studies in Religion